Library of
Davidson College

Mocking Epic

 *José Porrúa Turanzas, S.A.*

EDICIONES

Director General:
José Porrúa Venero

Sub-Director General:
Enrique Porrúa Venero

Director:
Constantino García Garvía

Asesor literario:
Bruno M. Damiani

studia humanitatis

Directed by
BRUNO M. DAMIANI
The Catholic University of America

Advisory Board

Juan Bautista Avalle-Arce
University of North Carolina

Theodore Beardsley
The Hispanic Society of America

Giovanni Maria Bertini
Università di Torino

Heinrich Bihler
Universität Göttingen

Harold Cannon
National Endowment
for the Humanities

Dante Della Terza
Harvard University

Frédéric Deloffre
Université de Paris-Sorbonne

Robert J. DiPietro
University of Delaware

Giovanni Fallani
Musei Vaticani

John E. Keller
University of Kentucky

Richard Kinkade
University of Connecticut

Juan M. Lope Blanch
Universidad Nacional Autónoma
de México

Leland R. Phelps
Duke University

Martín de Riquer
Real Academia Española

Joseph Silverman
University of California
(Santa Cruz)

Mocking Epic

Waltharius, Alexandreis
AND THE PROBLEM
OF CHRISTIAN HEROISM

BY
DENNIS M. KRATZ

studia humanitatis

PUBLISHER AND DISTRIBUTOR
José Porrúa Turanzas, S. A.
Cea Bermúdez, 10 - Madrid-3
ESPAÑA

NORTH AMERICAN DISTRIBUTION
1383 Kersey Lane
Potomac, Maryland 20854

© DENNIS M. KRATZ

Dep. legal M. 20.740.-1980

I. S. B. N. 84-7317-093-8

IMPRESO EN ESPAÑA
PRINTED IN SPAIN

*Ediciones José Porrúa Turanzas, S. A.
Cea Bermúdez, 10 - Madrid-3*

TALLERES GRÁFICOS PORRÚA, S. A.
JOSÉ, 10 - MADRID-29

for ABBY ROBINSON KRATZ
car a son avis n'en est nulle pareille a elle

ACKNOWLEDGMENTS

A portion of Chapter One appeared, in somewhat different form, as «Aeneas or Christ? An Epic Parody by Sedulius Scottus,» in *Classical World* Volume 69, Number 5 (1976). The analysis of the *Waltharius* in Chapter Two is a revised and expanded version of a discussion which forms part of my essay «Quid Waltharius Ruodliebque cum Christo?» in *The Epic in Medieval Society*, ed. Harald Scholler (Max Niemeyer Verlag: Tübingen, 1977). The translation from the *Nibelungenlied* at the beginning of Chapter Two is, slightly altered, that of A. T. Hatto (Penguin Books: Baltimore, Maryland, 1970 [1965]).

The writing of this book was aided by a grant-in-aid for research and an award of Assigned Research Duty during 1976 by the College of Humanities of the Ohio State University.

Table of Contents

	PAGE
PREFACE	xiii
1. Ramifications of Epic Heroism	1
2. Mocking the Hero: Walter of Aquitaine and the Sin of Greed	15
3. Mocking Heroism: Alexander the Great and the Pursuit of Glory	61
CONCLUSION: Irony and Christian Epic	157
APPENDIX: List of Editions	167
ANALYTICAL INDEX	169

Preface

In the present period of growing appreciation for medieval literature, the Latin epic poetry composed between the ninth and twelfth centuries remains largely ignored. There exists no comprehensive survey of Christian Latin epic; and all too little has been written, particularly in English, about specific poems. The *Waltharius*, for example, has rightly been praised as one of the finest literary monuments of the Carolingian era; moreover, it has been the subject of a considerable amount of discussion among German scholars; but it has inspired no complete book and a mere handful of articles in English. The neglect of Walter of Châtillon's *Alexandreis*, despite the enormous popularity and influence of that epic in the twelfth and thirteenth centuries, has been even more widespread. Not since 1917 has a book been devoted to the poem, and since then less than a half dozen studies of any consequence have appeared. Indeed, the most recent edition of the poem was published in 1863 and is not now generally accessible. (Professor Marvin Colker's critical edition of the *Alexandreis* will fill this gap.) Finally, as important as the neglect of these two poems is the fact that the previous analyses of them, while praiseworthy in many respects, have failed to make clear their essential character.

My primary goal in this book is the modest one of explicating two works which I admire and which I believe provide evidence of the continuing vitality of the classical tradition in medieval Europe. Its beginning lies in the question of how a medieval poet transforms a classical literary genre into a vehicle for the expression of a Christian theme. The idea of a comparative study devoted to the *Waltharius* and *Alexandreis* was first suggested by my discovery that their authors had arrived independently at the same solution to this problem; for both stress the inadequacy of the classical epic tradition for the depiction of Christian virtue, and both demonstrate that inadequacy by mocking the apparent heroes of their narratives. In addition, not only the nature but also the excellence of each epic is more readily discerned when it is considered beside the other.

Mocking Epic, then, explores one aspect of the Christian response to the literary heritage of classical antiquity. Its subject is the use of irony by two gifted poets to create narratives which are at once epic and Christian. The first chapter establishes a definition of irony as criticism expressed in language which seems to praise. The second and third chapters are close readings, respectively, of the *Waltharius* and *Alexandreis*. The former is shown to be an epic which belittles the values of the Germanic heroic code as founded on the sin of avarice; the latter attacks the pursuit of worldly fame which Walter of Châtillon regards as an essential component of the classical concept of heroic *virtus*. In each case, my interpretation emerges from an analysis of the poet's sustained use of allusions to works of both classical and Christian literature. A proper reading of the *Waltharius* depends partly on our recognition of a series of interrelated allusions to the *Aeneid*, the Bible, and Prudentius' *Psychomachia*. The first clue to Walter's negative attitude toward Alexander the Great is to be found in his use of Lucan's *Bellum Civile*, which contains a bitter denunciation of Alexander, as his primary epic model. Walter's attack upon the search for *gloria* to which Alexander devotes his life is effected through the carefully orchestrated use of references to Boethius' *De Consolatione Philosophiae*. My concluding chapter reviews the similarity in the solution of both poets to the problem of adapting the epic tradition to Christian purposes. In each poem, that solution lies not in the celebration of the *virtus* of any individual, but in the mockery of outmoded pagan heroic values.

It gives me pleasure to acknowledge the assistance which has generously been offered to me as I was preparing this book. I am especially grateful to Professors Mark Morford, Charles Babcock, Carl Schlam, and Stanley Kahrl for their constant support and sound advice. I thank also my colleagues in The Ohio State University's Center for Medieval and Renaissance Studies: no medievalist could have a more stimulating or congenial forum for the sharing of ideas. Professors Francis Newton, Theodore Andersson, Janet Martin, and F. P. Pickering have been kind enough to consider my work on epic poetry and respond with valuable suggestions. I was fortunate to begin my study of medieval Latin literature under the guidance of Professor Herbert Bloch, and to him I express my deep and abiding appreciation. My greatest debt —not only for her many perceptive comments and criticisms which have made this book better, but also for the patience, encouragement, and the gift of time which made it possible—is joyfully acknowledged in the dedication.

RAMIFICATIONS OF EPIC HEROISM

> ... cogebar Aeneae nescio cuius errores, oblitus errorum meorum, et plorare Didonem mortuam, quia se occidit ab amore, cum interea me ipsum in his a te morientem, deus, vita mea, siccis oculis ferrem miserrimus. Quid enim miserius misero non miserante se ipsum et flente Didonis mortem, quae fiebat amando Aenean, non flente autem mortem suam, quae fiebat non amando te, deus, lumen cordis mei et panis intus animae meae et virtus maritans mentem meam et sinum cogitationis meae?
> *Confessions* 13

The attempts of medieval poets to use classical literary genres for the expression of Christian values often reveal an ambivalent attitude toward pagan culture. Those authors, in particular, who composed epic poems in Latin modeled on the *Aeneid* and its successors were compelled to face the inherent conflict between the traditional concept of the epic hero and the standards of Christian ethics. In grappling with this problem many tried to forge a new definition of heroic virtue and managed, with varying degrees of success, to reconcile classical and Christian elements within the portrait of a single protagonist (1). In two works, however, the *Waltharius* and

---

(1) Examples include the panegyric epics concerning Charlemagne (*Karolus Magnus et Leo Papa*, s. 9), Henry IV (*Carmen de Bello Saxonico*, s. 11), and Frederick Barbarossa (*Ligurinus*, s. 12). Of particular interest is the *Ruodlieb* (s. 11). For discussion of this work as propounding Christian heroism, see Werner Braun, *Studien zum Ruodlieb* (Berlin, 1962), and my essay «Ruodlieb: Christian

Alexandreis, a radically different approach is taken to resolve the problem of transforming the epic into a Christian genre. The essential nature of both epics has eluded modern critics, who have rightly praised the poets' skillful imitation of their models but wrongly assumed their intention to be the celebration of heroic excellence; for although writing in very different circumstances and three centuries apart, the two poets—a ninth-century German monk and Walter of Châtillon, one of best known poets in twelfth-century France—make similar use of sustained irony to embed Christian meaning in their narratives. In Walter of Aquitaine and Alexander the Great each poem seems to possess a positive exemplar of *virtus;* but a closer look at the poet's subtle interweaving of classical and Christian references reveals that his real purpose is to attack the values associated with epic, and that the Christian theme of each narrative lies in the mockery, not the praise of its «hero.»

Criticism under the guise of praise is a form of irony, which classical and medieval sources alike define in general as «saying one thing but meaning another.» Quintilian discusses irony under the heading of *allegoria* (*Inst. Orat.* 8.6.44: [allegoria] aliud verbis aliud sensu ostendit), and asserts that in *ironia* the meaning is the opposite of the words (8.6.54: quo contraria ostenditur, ironia est). By employing irony the orator can criticize under a pretense of praise or praise with simulated blame (8.6.54: laudis adsimulatione detrahere et vituperationis laudare concessum est). This two-fold use is preserved in Isidore of Seville's definition (*Etymologiae* 2.21.41):

> ironia est, cum per simulationem diversum quam dicit intellegi cupit; fit autem cum laudamus eum

---

Epic Hero,» *Classical Folia* 27, Number 2 (1973): 252-266. Among the many works which deal with the general issue of the attitude of Christianity toward classical literature are W. Krause, *Die Stellung der frühchristlichen Autoren zur heidnischen Literatur* (Vienna, 1958), and H. Hagendahl, *Latin Fathers and the Classics* (Goteborg, 1958). Regarding Christian attacks on Aeneas, see Meyer Reinhold, «The Unhero Aeneas,» *Classica et Mediaevalia* 27 (1966): 195-207.

quem vituperare volumus, aut vituperamus quem laudare volumus; utriusque exemplum erit, si dicas «amatorem reipublicae» Catilinam, «hostem reipublicae» Scipionem.

In the Middle Ages as now, however, irony more often implied criticism couched in laudatory words (laudamus eum quem vituperare volumus). Cicero makes reference to the use of irony to express sarcasm (*Acad. Quaest.* 2.5.15), the aspect of the trope which is emphasized in the discussion by Donatus, the fourth-century Roman grammarian whose *Ars Grammatica* was enormously influential throughout the entire medieval period. Although his definition allows for both types of irony (3.6.30: ironia est tropus per contrarium quod conatur ostendens), the one example which he provides is the ironic reproach which Juno addresses to Venus for her action in using Cupid to inflame Dido with love for Aeneas (*Aeneid* 4.93-94: egregiam vero laudem et spolia ampla refertis/tuque puerque tuus). Moreover, *vituperatio* is the only use for ironic language which appears in a discussion found in the *Rhetorica Antiqua* by Boncompagno de Signa, a teacher of rhetoric and grammar at Bologna in the early thirteenth century (2). He defines irony as the use of words to convey disdain and ridicule (yronia enim est plana et demulcens verborum positio cum indignatione animi et subsannatione). To help his students he then provides a series of illustrations, among them praising a lecher for his chastity and a pauper for his riches (luxuriosum de castitate... pauperem de divitiis); and he concludes with a reminder that it is nothing but mockery to commend the evil deeds of someone through their opposite (nil aliud est vituperarium quam alicuius malefacta per contrarium commendare) (3).

For evidence of the recognition in the Middle Ages of ironic

---

(2) The excerpt is edited by John F. Benton as an appendix to his essay «Clio and Venus: An Historical View of Medieval Love,» in *The Meaning of Courtly Love*, ed. F. X. Newman (Albany, 1968), p. 37.

(3) For a useful discussion of the rhetorical theory of *ironia* and

language in epic such as that cited from the *Aeneid* by Donatus we can turn to the commentaries on Lucan's *De Bello Civili*. A gloss to 4.219 (ducibus quoque vita petita est?) explains that this question is framed *per ironiam*. Of greater consequence is the fact that commentators from the tenth century on regarded the invocation to Nero at the beginning of the epic as mockery. Through the twelfth century and beyond the interpretation that Lucan means his apparent praise to be taken ironically is, if not unanimous, predominant. The comments made by Arnulf of Orleans (*fl.* 1200) that Lucan is speaking ironically and derisively (sed hoc dicit oblique et derisorie...et hoc ironice) are typical. Indeed, when there occurs in one twelfth-century *accessus* the statement that the praise is sincere, a commentator adds, rather unkindly, «recte autem intelligentibus hic laus est vituperatio» (4).

It is fair to say, then, that there were medieval readers of epic who were not insensitive to ironic language; moreover, the evidence suggests that an author trained in rhetoric was likely to be aware of the technique of wording praise so that knowledgeable readers would recognize apparent *laudatio* as actual *vituperatio*. The employment by the best medieval poets of such veiled criticism, not only in isolated instances within a narrative but also as a strategy pervading the entire work, has in fact been gaining more and more attention in recent years (5). To find an example in Latin literature of an ironic

---

its implications for medieval narrative, see D. H. Green, «On Damning with Faint Praise in Medieval Literature,» *Viator*, Volume 6 (1975): 117-170.

(4) *Adnotationes Super Lucanum*, ed. I. Endt (Stuttgart, 1969 [1907]), p. 131. Berthe M. Marti discusses the commentaries in her article «Lucan's Invocation in the Light of the Medieval Commentaries,» *Quadrivium*, 1 (1956): 7-18.

(5) The seminal work is D. W. Robertson, Jr., *A Preface to Chaucer* (Princeton, 1962). See also D. H. Green, «Irony and Medieval Romance,» in *Arthurian Romance*, ed. D. D. R. Owen (New York, 1972), pp. 49-64. On Chrétien de Troyes cf. the comments by Owen, «Profanity and its Purpose in Chrétien's *Cliges* and *Lancelot*,» *ibid.*, p. 39: «...most of his work has an ambivalent quality: he is inclined to compose tongue-in-cheek, inviting us to take his story

stance sustained through an entire poem we need look no further, interestingly enough, than the satire *missus sum in vineam* by Walter of Châtillon, the author of the *Alexandreis*. In that poem Walter assumes the persona of a man who prefers money and pleasure to knowledge. On the surface, its twenty strophes comprise a denunciation of the pursuit of *virtus* in general and the study of literature in particular (6. str. 5):

> qui virtutes appetit, labitur in imum,
> querens sapientiam irruit in limum;
> imitetur igitur hec dicentem mimum:
> o cives, cives, querenda pecunia primum.

Walter seems to counsel the neglect of wisdom, which brings only ruin, and to exhort the reader, before he does anything else, to acquire wealth. But the poem is ironic. We have here, in Witke's apt phrase, a reverse satire; for Walter allows the persona to propound his views only in order to expose their absurdity and thus to evoke sympathy for the opposite position. This is a sophisticated mode of satire, which depends in part upon the use of classical and Christian allusions in such a way as to undercut the meaning of the statement in which they occur. As Witke has noted, it takes an educated audience to appreciate Walter's irony (6). We will see that a similar conclusion can be drawn concerning the mode not only of Walter's *Alexandreis* but also of the *Waltharius*, and concerning the kind of audience needed to enjoy the mockery of heroic epic to be found in them.

The notion of a Latin epic poet criticizing the very genre

---

seriously if we wish, but hinting that it would be more fun if we would share the secret joke he is playing on his heroes and heroines.» Of value too is Peter Haidu, *Aesthetic Distance in Chrétien de Troyes: Irony and Comedy in «Cliges» and «Perceval»* (Geneva, 1968), and R. G. Kunzer, *The Tristan of Gottfried von Strassburg: An Ironic Perspective* (Berkeley, 1973).

(6) For a detailed analysis both of this poem and of the role of irony in Walter's satires, see Charles Witke, *Latin Satire: The Structure of Persuasion* (Leiden, 1970), pp. 233-266.

which he is imitating is not unprecedented. Christian epic displayed from the beginning an antagonism toward the literary tradition from which it sprang. Juvencus, the first Latin poet to use epic as a vehicle for the presentation of Christian matter, even offers an *apologia* for his decision to recount the story of Christ in this manner. The passage deserves to be quoted in full (*Evang.* praefatio 1-27):

> immortale nihil mundi conpage tenetur,
> non orbis, non regna hominum, non aurea Roma,
> non mare, non tellus, non ignea sidera caeli.
> nam statuit genitor rerum inrevocabile tempus,
> quo cunctum torrens rapiat flamma ultima mundum.
> sed tamen innumeros homines sublimia facta
> et virtutis honos in tempora longa frequentant,
> adcumulant quorum famam laudesque poetae.
> hos celsi cantus, Smyrnae de fonte fluentes,
> illos Minciadae celebrat dulcedo Maronis.
> nec minor ipsorum discurrit gloria vatum,
> quae manet aeternae similis, dum saecla volabunt
> et vertigo poli terras atque aequora circum
> aethera sidereum iusso moderamine volvet.
> quod si tam longam meruerunt carmina famam,
> quae veterum gestis hominum mendacia nectunt,
> nobis certa fides aeternae in saecula laudis
> immortale decus tribuet meritumque rependet.
> nam mihi carmen erit Christi vitalia gesta,
> divinum populis falsi sine crimine donum.
> nec metus, ut mundi rapiant incendia secum
> hoc opus; hoc etenim forsan me subtrahet igni
> tunc, cum flammivoma descendet nube coruscans
> iudex, altithroni genitoris gloria, Christus.
> ergo age, sanctificus adsit mihi carminis auctor
> spiritus, et puro mentem riget amne carentis
> dulcis Jordanis, ut Christo digna loquamur.

Juvencus' words serve a dual purpose. By praising Homer's lofty songs (celsi cantus Smyrnae de fonte fluentes) and the sweetness of Vergil (dulcedo Maronis), Juvencus announces his intention to compose within the bounds of the epic genre. At the same time, he is conscious of the superiority of his new subject. The opening stress upon the impermanence of the created universe (inmortale nihil mundi conpage tenetur) establishes the transitory nature of the glory which pagan epics can achieve (gloria vatum); for though such praise may have the appearance of permanence (aeternae similis), the next phrase (dum saecla volabunt) reminds us of its connection with the ephemeral world. In contrast to the transitory fame gained by celebrating the deeds of men (veterum gestis hominum), Juvencus will gain eternal praise (nobis certa fides aeternae in saecula laudis/immortale decus tribuet) by celebrating the living deeds of Christ (Christi vitalia gesta). Those deeds are both «living» and «life giving,» for telling them will perhaps save Juvencus at the Last Judgment. The work at least will escape the flames, as the lies (mendacia) of the *Aeneid* surely will not. Juvencus concludes the preface on a note to which we will return, a contrast between the true glory (altithroni genitoris gloria) with which epic poetry should be concerned and the lesser glory won by poets (gloria vatum) who celebrate earthly achievements. His *apologia* complete, the poet can now offer a Christian version of the epic invocation (sanctificus adsit mihi carminis auctor/spiritus) and proceed with his narrative (7).

In addition to such direct criticism, Latin epic generated parodies of itself; and among the burlesques of the tradition is a delightful short poem, composed in the mid-ninth century by Sedulius Scottus, which draws its humor from the difficulty of creating a protagonist who is at once a «Christian» and an «epic» hero (8). In this narrative, generally referred to as the

---

(7) A discussion of the concern of Christian poets with the propriety of using the epic genre appears in Barbara Lewalski, *Milton's Brief Epic* (Providence, R. I., 1966); the issue is treated with insight in Macklin Smith, *Prudentius' Psychomachia: a Reexamination* (Princeton, 1976).

(8) Two other brief parodies are Theodulf of Orleans' *De Pugna Avium*, which I discuss in an essay forthcoming in *Latomus*, and

De Quodam Verbece, we will see at work some of the same undercutting techniques employed in the *Waltharius* and *Alexandreis.*

The story concerns a ram who is set upon and eventually killed by a pack of dogs. In a sense, Sedulius has produced a gruesome comedy of errors, for the dogs attack the ram under the mistaken impression that he is the accomplice of a robber who has just victimized them. Although outnumbered, the ram at first stands his ground and even puts the dogs momentarily to flight. In true epic fashion he then delivers a speech not only proclaiming his innocence but also swearing a mighty oath—on his head, his horns, and his proud forehead (73-74: per caput hoc iuro, per cornua perque superbam/hanc frontem vobis)—to defeat the attackers if they persist against him. Although the other dogs seem convinced, their leader, Cerberus by name, arouses them to renew the fray. In this battle also the ram gains a momentary advantage; however, incautious with success, he gets tangled in some thorn-bushes and is killed by Cerberus.

The scene outlined above clearly is intended as a parody of an epic combat. Sedulius employs not only the themes but also the language of the Latin epic tradition. One passage, for example, crams into three lines variations on «noise» topoi (54-56) (9):

> ingens fit strepitus, fit sonus atque fragor;
> oribus et rapidis furem furtumque requirit:
> frondea silva latrat, personat omne nemus.

Sedulius has, moreover, sprinkled his narrative with allusions

---

an anonymous poem from the eleventh century entitled *Altercatio Nani et Leporis.* See also my «Aeneas or Christ? An Epic Parody by Sedulius Scottus,» *Classical World,* Volume 69, Number 5 (1976): 319-323.

(9) For a discussion of these topoi and their integration into conventional epic battle scenes, see Pierre-Jean Miniconi, *Index des thèmes 'guerriers' de la poesie epique latine* (Paris, 1951).

specifically to the *Aeneid*. Consider the beginning of the ram's speech to his pursuers (65-68):

> «quis furor in vestris consurgit cordibus?» inquit,
> «gnoscite me famulum praesulis Hartgarii.
> non sum latro malus, non sum furunculus ille,
> sed sum multo pius, dux gregis eximius.»

The *multo* is here a classical hero in animal skin whose words *sum multo pius* could hardly fail to call Aeneas to mind (*Aeneid* 1.378: sum pius Aeneas). Moreover, the language which Sedulius uses to describe the ram's death is drawn from the *Aeneid* (99-100):

> labitur exanimis multo, mirabile visu
> irrorans vepres sanguine purpureo.

Mirabile visu needs no explanation. *Labitur exanimis purpureo* recalls the death of Arruns in the *Aeneid* (11.818-819):

> labitur exsanguis, labuntur frigida leto
> lumina, purpureus quondam color ora relinquit.

Finally, the phrase *irrorans vepres sanguine* is an echo of the death of Tullus as depicted on the shield of Aeneas (8.645: et sparsi rorabant sanguine vepres).

Side by side with these obvious Vergilian reminiscences, however, Sedulius has placed allusions to the Bible which suggest that the *multo* is meant to be a Christian martyr as well as an epic hero. Are the briars sprinkled with blood meant also to recall Christ's crown of thorns (Matthew 27-29: coronam de spinis)? More certain is the Christian symbolism of the dogs who are the ram's tormentors; for in Psalm 21, which was commonly interpreted as the prophetic expression of Christ's words during the Passion, the Psalmist describes himself as surrounded by dogs (Psalm 21.17: circumdederunt me canes multi). Let us examine, moreover, Sedulius' description of the actual robber who in effect caused the ram's death (43-48):

> quidam latro fuit nequam de gente Goliae
> Aethiopum similis, Cacus et arte malus,
> terribilis forma vultu piceusque maligno,
> asper erat factis, asper et eloquiis:
> te, pie multo, tulit, manibus traxitque nefandis
> per multos tribulos, heu nefas, o miserum.

The *latro* is from the race of Goliath (de gente Goliae); and his blackness (Aethiopum similis, vultu piceusque maligno) suggests him as a figure of the Devil. The notion of a robber's compelling the ram to undergo tribulations (te...traxit... / per multos tribulos) implies that the entire narrative may be an extended allusion to the parable of the Good Samaritan (Luke 10.29-37), which begins «a man was going down from Jerusalem to Jericho, and he fell among robbers (incidit in latrones).» Sedulius strengthens this implication by beginning the description of the ram's entanglement in the thorn-bushes—the immediate cause of his death—with the words *incidit in tribulos* (10).

Further Christian coloring occurs in the *planctus* (105-132) which follows the narrative. There Sedulius addresses the ram in terms more appropriate to a martyr than to a fallen warrior. The ram is *simplex, sine fraude maligna* (105). He is not avaricious, but content with plain food, drink, and clothing; nor is he proud (113-114):

> nonque superbus equo lustrabat amoena virecta,
> sed propriis pedibus rite migrabat iter.

To define his humility in terms of walking instead of riding may at first seem odd, since rams so rarely ride horses anyway; but the line of course is a reference (humorous in its incon-

---

(10) St. Jerome, *Commentarioli in Psalmos*: in ps. xxi. 2, *Corpus Christianorum*, Series Latina 72 (Turnholt, 1967), p. 198; see James Marrow, «*Circumdederunt me canes multi*: Christ's Tormentors in Northern European Art of the Late Middle Ages and Early Renaissance,» *The Art Bulletin*, Volume 59, Number 2 (1977): 167-181.

gruity?) to the conventional image of Superbia on her horse as depicted in the *Psychomachia* (178-181). There follow, at any rate, two explicit comparisons of the ram with Christ (117-122):

> agnus ut altithronus pro peccatoribus acrem
>   gustavit mortem filius ipse dei
> carpens mortis iter canibus laceratus iniquis
>   pro latrone malo sic, pie multo, peris
> quomodo pro Isaac aries sacer hostia factus:
>   sic tu pro misero victima grata manes.

The first simile compares the death of the ram to that of Christ. The second makes use of the common typological reference of the ram sacrificed in place of Isaac. Sedulius concludes the *planctus* with a reminder that Christ forgave a *latro* while suffering on the cross, thus drawing our attention back to Christ as the teller of the parable of the Good Samaritan.

In addition to including in his portrait of the ram elements which are identifiably either Christian or classical, Sedulius makes use of purposefully ambiguous allusions. I have mentioned, for example, the two possible reminiscences of the phrase *irrorans vepres sanguine*; and while the dogs may be easily understood as Christ's tormentors, nevertheless they have names drawn from pagan mythology: the leader is Cerberus, and the phrase *Cacus et arte malus* is meant also to evoke the monster whom Hercules defeats. Even more significant is the ambiguous mingling of epic and Biblical references in the description of the ram himself. In one instance Sedulius is guilty of contradictory statements about his hero; for although in the *planctus* Sedulius praises his humility, earlier the ram had sworn an oath *per superbam hanc frontem*. Moreover, the adjective *pius,* which Sedulius applies five times to the ram, reinforces the ambiguity. The use of *pius* in the phrase *sum multo pius* (68) without question links the heroic ram to Aeneas. The *furor* which earlier in the same speech the ram attributes to his enemies (65: quis furor in vestris consurgit cordibus?) even recalls the basic *pietas/furor* dichotomy of the

Aeneid. On the other hand, the phrase *sic, pie multo, peris* (120) can have nothing to do with Aeneas, sandwiched as it is by the two explicit comparisons of the ram with Christ.

A sometimes self-contradictory amalgam of classical and Christian elements, the *multo pius* is an animal version of Walter of Aquitaine and Alexander the Great; and Sedulius' poem works on much the same kind of irony which we will see in the *Waltharius* and *Alexandreis*. The ram is set up as a heroic figure, but inconsistencies within the portrait alert the careful reader to the possibilities of a concealed purpose. That purpose is ridicule. The ram is, in part, an alter Aeneas; he is, in part, another Christ; in the end he is, completely, dinner (133-140):

> tu, bone multo, vale, nivei gregis inclite ductor,
>   heu quia nec vivum te meus hortus habet.
> forsan, amice, tibi fieret calidumque lavacrum—
>   non alia causa, iure sed hospitii;
> ipse ministrassem devoto pectore limphas
>   cornigero capiti, calcibus atque tuis
> te (fateor) cupii; viduam matremque cupisco
>   fratres atque tuos semper amabo. vale.

The whole poem, we now realize, is in praise of the main course of a meal. The statement of love and desire at the end of the *planctus* (te...cupii...cupisco / ...semper amabo) reflects the language with which Sedulius had lauded the ram at the beginning of the «epic» (15-16):

> iuro per digitos, quod in hoc non mentior umquam:
>   tales quod cupio, diligo, semper amo.

The fingers on which Sedulius is swearing his oath are holding the roasted meat! Our knowledge now of this fact casts a mocking light on the ram's heroic declaration of victory over the dogs (73: per caput hoc iuro). I need hardly add that the love which Sedulius declares is carnal.

Sedulius, then, has exploited the problem of portraying a

Christian hero without attacking the concept itself. The *De Quodam Verbece* is a sustained ironic narrative which sets up the ram first as a hero then as a martyr only to undercut that portrait by revealing him as dinner; but Sedulius offers no message beyond a warning against underestimating his cleverness. For mockery with a more serious goal we must now turn to the *Waltharius*.

MOCKING THE HERO: WALTER OF AQUITAINE AND THE SIN OF GREED

> Des antwurte Hiltbrant:
> «zwiu verwizet ir mir daz?
> nû wer was, der ûfem schilde
> vor dem Wasgensteine saz,
> dô im von Spanje Walther
> sô vil der mâge sluoc?
> ouch habt ir noch ze zeigen
> an iu selben genuoc.»
>
> (Hildebrand replied: «Why do you reproach me with that? Who sat on his shield below the Waskenstein while Walter of Spain slew so many of his kinsmen? You yourself are not above reproach.»)
> *Nibelungenlied* 2281

As can be said about Carolingian culture in general, the *Waltharius* is a mixture of three main elements—Germanic, Christian, and classical. Its story and characters are drawn from the same body of legends which was to produce the *Nibelungenlied*. Indeed, the *Nibelungenlied* contains three separate references to events recounted in the *Waltharius*—two to the time which Walter and Hagen spend in the service of Attila (1756: canto 28; 1797: canto 29) and one to Hagen's initial refusal to fight against Walter at Waskenstein (2281: canto 39). The extent to which that legend is turned into a Christian tale is a matter of considerable dispute for which this chapter provides the solution. For the moment it is enough to say that the poem was almost certainly composed by a monk, since the first line is addressed to his *fratres,* and that it concludes with a Christian prayer (1456):

haec est Waltharii poesis. vos salvet Iesus.

As for the classical element, the author of the *Waltharius* clearly saw himself as a continuator of the Latin epic tradition. The narrative reveals his familiarity, in particular, with three epics: the *Aeneid, Thebaid* and *Psychomachia.* Given this three-part nature of the epic, I must raise the critical issue: To what extent, if at all, was the poet able to weld these disparate components into a unified and meaningful whole?

Although the question of the poet's ability to reconcile these three elements is in part responsible for the extensive amount of criticism which the *Waltharius* has engendered over the past century (1), uncertainty as to when and by whom it was written has provided an equal incitement to research and controversy. I take the position that the *Waltharius* was composed in the mid-ninth century, and my inclination is to accept the claim of authorship which a certain Gerald advances in a 22-line preface to the epic. If, as may be the case, Gerald was not the monk who composed the epic, we must at least grant him, I will show, the honor of being the first critic to perceive the true nature of this remarkable narrative (2).

---

(1) For a survey of *Waltharius* criticism see Otto Schumann, «Waltharius-Literatur seit 1926,» *Anzeiger für deutsches Altertum* 65 (1951-1952): 13-41; a full bibliography and a collection of important essays be found in Emil Ernst Ploss, ed., *Waltharius und Walthersage: Eine Dokumentation der Forschung* (Hildesheim, 1969). Recent studies not included in either of the bibliographic surveys mentioned above are as follows: Peter Dronke, «Functions of Classical Borrowing in Medieval Latin,» in R. R. Bolgar, ed., *Classical Influences on European Culture: AD 500-900* (Cambridge, 1971), pp. 159-164; Karl Langosch, *Waltharius: Die Dichtung und die Forschung* (Darmstadt, 1973); Rosemarie Katscher, «Waltharius—Dichtung und Dichter,» *Mittellateinisches Jahrbuch* 9 (1976): 48-120; Theodore Andersson, *Early Epic Scenery* (Ithaca, N. Y., 1976), pp. 131-144; and my «Quid Waltharius Ruoliebque cum Christo?» in Harald Scholler, ed., *The Epic in Medieval Society* (Tübingen, 1977), pp. 126-149.

(2) On this issue see Langosch, *op. cit.* Basic studies are by Jacob Grimm and Andreas Schmeller, *Lateinische Gedichte des X. und XI Jahrhunderts* (Göttingen, 1838); Rudolf Reeh, «Zur Frage nach dem Verfasser des Waltharliedes,» *Zeitschrift für deutsche*

Two issues have long dominated the criticism directed at the *Waltharius* as a work of art: Gerald's skill in recreating the epic genre and the degree to which, if at all, he has created an epic which is Christian in spirit. On the first issue there is now general agreement; but the second still evokes argument. Some find the poem to be essentially, even totally Christian (3).

Philologie 51 (1926): 413-431; Karl Strecker, ed., *Waltharius* (Berlin, 1947), pp. 7-20; Otto Schumann, «Zum Waltharius,» *Zeitschrift für deutsches Altertum* 83 (1951): 30-35; Wolfram von den Steinen, «Der Waltharius und sein Dichter, *ZfdA* 84 (1952): 1-47.

It was once assumed that the *Waltharius* was composed in the tenth century by Ekkehard I. The identification of Ekkehard as the poet was first offered by Grimm on the basis of a statement by Ekkehard IV, in the eleventh century chronicle *Casus s. Galli*, that while a schoolboy the earlier Ekkehard had composed an exercise entitled *vitam Waltharii manu fortis*, which he had then revised and polished. This view was first challenged by Reeh, who suggested that Gerald, the author of a 22-line dedication to a *Pontifex* Erkambald which precedes the poem in several manuscripts, was also the author of the epic. Reeh, however, agreed with the tenth century dating, since he identified Erkambald with the man of that name who was bishop at Strassburg from 965-991. To Strecker belongs the credit for proposing a new date. In his 1947 edition of the *Waltharius* he offered strong evidence that the poem was composed in the ninth century, although he rejected Gerald as the author. Since then, the idea of the *Waltharius* as a product of the ninth century has gained wide acceptance. Schumann, for example, showed that while the author quotes many classical and Christian sources, no citation is to an author later than 900. He argued that a late ninth-century date is most likely, since he accepted Gerald as the poet and identified Erkambald as a bishop in Eichstätt from *ca*. 880-912. Von den Steinen, on the other hand, would place the epic sometime between the *termini* 835-860. His argument for an earlier date in the ninth century is based partly on certain weaknesses in Schumann's case for Erkambald of Eichstätt and partly on the nature of various historical references within the poem— especially the designation of Metz as a *metropolis* and Châlon as the capital of Burgundy. The controversy still rages; but attempts to place the poem later than the ninth century and/or to disprove Gerald's claim to authorship are not convincing. Two recent efforts of this sort are Dieter Schaller, «Geraldus und St. Gallen—Zum Widmungsgedicht des Waltharius,» *Mittellateinisches Jahrbuch* 2 (1965): 74-84; and Hedwig Krammer, *Die Verfasserfrage des Waltharius* (Vienna, 1973).

(3) This interpretation was first offered by Hennig Brinkmann, «Ekkehards Waltharius als Kunstwerk,» *Zeitschrift für deutsche*

Others contend that the Christian references in the poem are inconsequential, and at least one critic has proclaimed the ethos of the *Waltharius* to be «hardly Christian at all» (4). An important recent development in *Waltharius* studies has been a growing appreciation of the poem's comic aspects (5). We will see, however, that humor through the use of mockery and irony, for from being a peripheral element of Gerald's epic technique, is in fact central to the design and Christian meaning of his narrative.

Gerald's mocking sense of humor is apparent even in his imitation of his epic models. That the *Waltharius* is conceived as a part of the continuum of the Latin epic tradition is indisputable. Gerald's language is rich in borrowings from the *Aeneid* and *Thebaid,* and the influence of Prudentius cannot be overemphasized. More important, Gerald demonstrates his knowledge, not just of specific models, but of the conventions of form and content associated more generally with the genre itself. It is interesting to note, though the fact has been

---

Bildung 43 (1928): 625-636. It is accepted by, among others, Schumann, von den Steinen, and Katscher.

(4) This view, first argued by Grimm, has recently been seconded by George F. Jones, «The Ethos of the *Waltharius*,» in *Middle Ages, Reformation, Volkskunde: Festschrift for John G. Kunstmann* (Chapel Hill, North Carolina, 1959), pp. 1-20; he writes (p. 7) «In view of ... the apparent superficiality of the Christian elements in the poem, I cannot agree with von den Steinen when he says that the *Waltharius* is entirely Christian even if not monastic in any one trait. Perhaps it would be better to say that the poem is monastic in many traits but hardly Christian at all.» For a similar assumption that the *Waltharius* is at best only superficially Christian, see Michael Cherniss, *Ingeld and Christ* (The Hague, 1972), esp. pp. 122-123. For an unfortunate example of the influence of the notion that the poem was the exercise of a school boy, consider the remark by Bernard F. Huppé, «The Concept of the Hero in the Early Middle Ages,» in *Concepts of the Hero in the Middle Ages and the Renaissance*, ed. Norman T. Burns and Christopher J. Regan (Albany, N. Y., 1975), p. 1: «... the *Waltharius* is an academic exercise which cannot seriously be considered as a work of art.»

(5) See Dronke, *op. cit.*; F. P. Pickering, *Augustinus oder Boethius?* II. Darstellender Band (Philologische Studien und Quellen: Berlin, 1976), pp. 119-122; Katscher, *op. cit.*, pp. 119-120.

ignored by those who deny Gerald's claim to authorship, that while the narrative itself lacks the conventional invocation and proposition, the preface contains both (prol. 1-4...17-18). In examining Gerald's *imitatio* I will look specifically at one simile which is representative of his careful artistry, at his handling of battle scenes, and at his description of a banquet.

Of the eight similes which occur in the *Waltharius,* the last and longest shows Gerald's skill to its fullest advantage (1337-1343):

> haud aliter, Numidus quam dum venabitur ursus
> et canibus circumdatus astat et artubus horret
> et caput occultans submurmurat ac propiantes
> amplexans Umbros miserum mutire coartat,
> —tum rabidi cirmumlatrant hinc inde Molossi
> comminus ac dirae metuunt accedere belvae—,
> taliter in nonam conflictus fluxerat horam.

This comparison of Walter to a wild bear surrounded by dogs emphasizes the desperate situation of the hero as he fights against Hagen and Gunther. The apparent source for the simile is Vergil's comparison of Mezentius to a wild boar harassed by hunting dogs who nonetheless are afraid to venture too near the angered beast (*Aeneid* 10.707-715). However, the image in the *Waltharius* includes the picture, not found in the *Aeneid,* of the wild beast surrounded by dogs (canibus circumdatus). Gerald is playing, of course, on the same image of Christ's tormentors as dogs to which Sedulius alludes; but the irony of any linking of Walter to Christ at this point in the narrative will soon be clear. I would add, finally, that in composing this simile Gerald seems also to have had the *Thebaid* in mind. In Statius' epic, the climactic battle in which Eteocles and Polynices kill each other contains a simile likening the two brothers to enraged boars (11.530-538). The image of the two animals locked in mortal combat signals the fulfillment of a prophetic vision in which a Bacchant sees two bulls fighting to the death (4.396-400). The same pattern occurs in the *Waltharius,* for there too the animal image of the simile serves to fulfill the symbolic language of a prophetic vision. That prophecy is a dream in which Hagen sees a bear rip out his eye and some teeth after it has bitten off Gunther's leg (617-627):

> tunc Hagano ad regem: «porrectam suscipe gazam,
> hac potis es decorare, pater, tecum comitantes,
> et modo de pugna palmam revocare memento.
> ignotus tibi Waltharius et maxima virtus.
> ut mihi praeterita portendit visio nocte,
> non, si conserimus, nos prospera cuncta sequentur.
> visum quippe mihi te colluctarier urso,
> qui post conflictus longos tibi mordicus unum
> crus cum poplite ad usque femur decerpserat omne
> et mox auxilio subeuntem ac tela ferentem
> me petit atque oculum cum dentibus eruit unum.»

Such indeed will be the outcome of the struggle. Gerald underscores the connection between the wounds inflicted by the «bear» and those about to be inflicted by Walter when he concludes the simile with a reference to the length of the combat (in nonam conflictus fluxerat horam), thus picking up Hagen's reference to the long struggle (post conflictus longos) before the bear prevailed. Gerald, then, has imaginatively taken an image from the *Aeneid,* changed the animal involved, added a pertinent Biblical allusion, and made the recurrence of the imagery of a vision in the simile resemble the pattern found in the *Thebaid.* The artistry is admirable; and Gerald's decision to reinforce the correctness and importance of Hagen's vision with an extended simile provokes a question of no little importance: Why is the poet so insistent upon our foreknowledge of the result, or part of the result, of the climactic battle of his epic?

Scenes of fighting are an important part of the *Waltharius* and illustrate Gerald's broad based approach to imitation. Consider the first description of the advancing Hunnish army (40-63):

> namque Avares firma cum Francis pace peracta
> suspendunt a fine quidem regionis eorum.
> Attila sed celeres mox huc deflectit habenas,
> nec tardant relique satrapae vestigia adire.
> ibant aequati numero, sed et agmine longo,
> quadrupedum cursu tellus concussa gemebat.
> scutorum sonitu pavidus superintonat aether.
> ferrea silva micat totos rutilando per agros:
> haud aliter primo quam pulsans aequora mane
> pulcher in extremis renitet sol partibus orbis.
> iamque Ararim Rodanumque amnes transiverat altos
> atque ad praedandum cuneus dispergitur omnis.
> forte Cabillonis sedit Heriricus, et ecce
> attollens oculos speculator vociferatur:
> «quaenam condenso consurgit pulvere nubes?
> vis inimica venit, portas iam claudite cunctas!»
> iam tum, quid Franci fecissent, ipse sciebat
> princeps et cunctos compellat sic seniores:
> «si gens tam fortis, cui nos similare nequimus,
> cessit Pannoniae, qua nos virtute putatis
> huic conferre manum et patriam defendere dulcem?
> est satius, pactum faciant censumque capessant.
> unica nata mihi, quam tradere pro regione
> non dubito; tantum pergant, qui foedera firment.»

The scene is carefully structured. Our attention is focused first on Attila, who leads the advance. To emphasize the might of the approaching force Gerald makes use of the topoi of the «groaning earth» (tellus concussa gemebat) and the «resounding sky» (superintonat aether). He then describes the glitter of weapons in the sunlight (47-49) before offering a second statement of movement (50-51). Gerald then changes the perspective from a panoramic view to that of the watchman of the besieged city, who sees the cloud of dust which the army is raising (54-55). The device of the question (quaenam condenso consurgit pulvere nubes?) and its connection with the cloud of dust are from the *Aeneid* (9.36-38):

> quis globus, o cives, caligine volvitur atra?
> ferte citi ferrum, date tela, ascendite muros,
> hostis adest, heia!

But whereas Vergil then describes the preparations for battle within the Trojan camp, Gerald keeps his focus restricted to the individual; for Prince Hereric then summons his advisers and comes to a decision to submit to Attila. Legates are sent to the Hun; and the scene concludes, as it began, with Attila, the reentry of Attila serving as a transition to the next scene, the subjugation of Aquitaine.

Two features of Gerald's narrative technique are evident in this brief scene. First, he alternates the viewpoint from which the action is presented, and thus prevents the scene from becoming static. Second, he narrows the focus of the action, beginning with a panoramic view of the action and concluding with the observations and reactions of a specific individual. The next battle scene (170-214) has a similar design. When report of a rebellious tribe reaches Attila, he turns the conduct of affairs over to Walter, who musters the army. Upon reaching the battle field, he deploys his force, and this deployment is presented from his perspective (180: ecce locum pugnae conspexerat). Gerald then switches back to a panoramic view. The fighting begins. Unlike the first scene, here weapons are released, and to describe them Gerald again turns to commonplaces from the epic tradition (185-189):

> continuoque hastae volitant hinc indeque densae.
> fraxinus et cornus ludum miscebat in unum,
> fulminis inque modum cuspis vibrata micabat.
> ac veluti boreae sub tempore nix glomerata
> spargitur, haud aliter saevas iecere sagittas.

In this scene Gerald, always careful to vary his descriptions, employs the glitter topos with regard to weapons in flight rather than as part of the preparations for the fighting. The comparison of flying missiles to a storm is another commonplace; the image of snow may come from the *Aeneid* (11.610-

611: fundunt simul undique tela / crebra nivis ritu), but the use of a simile to emphasize the storm of weapons has numerous precedents (cf. *Aeneid* 9.668-671 and *Thebaid* 7.409-412). Gerald now gradually restricts the focus of his narrative. A general picture of hand-to-hand fighting (190-195) is followed by emphasis upon Walter's personal exploits (196-202). The rout completed, the Hunnish soldiers return home. Gerald repeats his practice of the previous battle episode by concluding with his focus on the individual, in this case Walter, with whom the scene began (214: sed ad solium mox Waltharius properavit), and using this device as a transition to the next scene.

Andersson's perceptive analysis of this scene shows how well Gerald has learned the composition of an epic battle (6). He employs, to be sure, specific Vergilian allusions and the commonplaces expected in descriptions of fighting; but it is the overall design of the scene that is most impressive. He sets the scene before the action begins, then alternates the depiction of mass movements with individual feats to keep the narrative lively. Moreover, he keeps our attention by gradually narrowing the focus of the scene. We are first given a view of the whole battlefield, then of the two armies as they approach one another, then of hand-to-hand combat, and finally of the exploits of a single warrior (7).

The longest battle scene in the epic describes Walter's confrontation with his Frankish assailants in the Vosges Mountains (644-1088). Others have dealt with Gerald's broad based imitation of epic models and the careful structuring of this scene; but another aspect of his artistry, the use of a clustering of allusions to a specific model, has gone unnoticed. Panzer,

---

(6) Andersson, *op. cit.*, pp. 133-137.
(7) See Hans Wagner, *Ekkehard und Vergil: Eine Vergleichende Interpretation der Kampfschilderungen im Waltharius*, Quellen und Studien zur Geschichte und Kultur des Altertums und des Mittelalters, Reihe D: Untersuchungen und Mitteilungen 9 (Heidelberg, 1939), *passim*; Andersson, *op. cit.*, pp. 137-144; Miniconi, *op. cit.*

to be sure, observed the similarities between this scene and the ambush of Tydeus in the *Thebaid* (2.496-743), but drew false conclusions from that resemblance (8). An episode in which a single warrior fights alone against overwhelming odds is, after all, a traditional motif of epic; and Gerald makes verbal allusions seven times to another example of this motif, the attack by Turnus upon the Trojan camp as recounted in the ninth book of the *Aeneid*. The implication of these interconnected allusions deserves mention.

The first six echoes all occur in the description of individual combats. Gerald makes the first of these doubly obvious. Before Walter kills Werinhard, he scornfully replies to the boasting of the Frankish warrior (742):

olli Waltharius ridenti pectore adorsus.

This is an echo of the statement by Turnus to the Trojan Pandarus before killing him (*Aeneid* 9.740: olli subridens sedato pectore Turnus). And Werinhard—as Gerald informs us at some length (726-729)—is the descendent of Pandarus. The scene from the *Aeneid* in which Turnus kills Pandarus is evoked twice more by Gerald. After Turnus speaks, Pandarus tries without success to wound him with a spear (*Aeneid* 9.743-744):

...ille rudem nodis et cortice crudo
intorquet summis adnixus viribus hastam.

Gerald calls this passage to mind when Batavrid throws his spear at Walter (888-889):

---

(8) Friedrich Panzer, *Der Kampf am Wasichenstein* (Speyer am Rhein, 1948) argues that the *Waltharius* is an original story concocted from episodes from the *Thebaid* and Ovid's *Metamorphoses*. For a rebuttal of the notion, as well as a masterful approach to the study of *imitatio* in the *Waltharius*, see Karl Stackmann, «Antike Elemente im Waltharius,» *Euphorion* 45 (1950): 231-248.

> dixit et in verbo nodosam destinat hastam,
> cuspide quam propria divertens transtulit heros.

In the *Aeneid,* when Pandarus' spear falls harmlessly to the ground, Turnus exclaims (9.747-748):

> at non hoc telum, mea quod vi dextera versat
> effugies, neque enim is teli nec vulneris auctor.

This phrase will later be echoed by the Frank Hadaward before he attacks Walter (797-798):

> ...neque enim is teli seu vulneris auctor.
> audi consilium, parmam deponito pictam.

In addition, the fight between Walter and this Hadaward includes two other references to Turnus' *aristeia*. Inside the Trojan camp, Turnus is attacked from every side, and stones resound as they strike his helmet (9.808-809: strepit adsiduo.../ tinnitu galea). Likewise the helmets of Walter and Hadaward resound (828: dant tinnitus galeae). Gerald then describes Hadaward's death (842: ille cadit, clipeus superintonat ingens) with a phrase used by Vergil with reference to Turnus' victim Bitias (9.709: clipeum intonat ingens). The last of these six evocations occurs, in both epics, when the single warrior is under attack by a group of enemies. Turnus' perspiration flows like a river (9.812-814):

> ...tum toto corpore sudor
> liquitur et piceum (nec respirare potestas)
> flumen agit.

Similarly rivers of sweat (999: manarunt cunctis sudoris flumina membris) pour from the bodies of Walter and his foes.

The force of these allusions is to link Walter with Turnus, a connection which Gerald's final reminiscence reinforces. Gunther, after losing all the men whom he sent against Walter, tries to goad Hagen into action by pointing to the disgrace which Walter—one man (ab uno)—has inflicted on the Frankish army (1084-1088):

> non modicum patimur damnum de caede virorum,
> dedecus at tantum superabit Francia numquam.
> antea quis fuimus suspecti, sibila dantes
> «Francorum» dicent «exercitus omnis ab uno,
> proh pudor ignotum vel quo, est impune necatus!»

This passage certainly reflects the values of the Germanic heroic code; however, the immediately identifiable source for Gunther's words is the same episode in the *Aeneid*; for they are based on Mnestheus' rebuke to the Trojans (9.783-787) in which he bemoans the shame (9.787: miseretque pudetque) brought on the Trojan army by one man (9.783: unus homo). The connection seems clear. As before, Gerald's poetic technique raises a question, in this instance concerning the aptness of comparing Walter, if he is meant to be a positive exemplar of Christian heroism, to Turnus.

In addition to the broader type of imitation reflected in his battle descriptions, Gerald includes one episode, the banquet given by Walter as part of his escape plan, based on a specific scene in the *Aeneid*. His model, of course, is the banquet which Dido gives in honor of Aeneas (1.637-756). A comparative look at the structure of the two episodes will reveal Gerald's imitative intent. Vergil's scene begins with a brief description of the sumptuously appointed banquet hall. There follows a digression which explains Venus' plan to use the event for her own purposes. On the day of the feast the guests—especially Aeneas and Cupid (as Iulus)—arrive. After much feasting the tables are removed and wine bowls brought in, at which time Dido offers a toast. After a song by Iopas, Dido makes her request for Aeneas to recount the story of his wanderings. In the *Waltharius* Gerald combines the first two elements of Vergil's scene; for Walter explains his ulterior motive while ordering Hiltgunt to make preparations for the banquet. On the appointed day the guests—especially Attila—

arrive, and Gerald takes this opportunity to describe the banquet hall. After much eating and drinking the tables are removed; and Walter offers a toast. In the *Waltharius* there follows more drinking, until all the Huns pass out.

In addition to following the basic structure of his Vergilian model, Gerald includes pointed verbal allusions to it. Consider Vergil's descriptions of the preparations for the feasting (1.637-642):

> at domus interior regali splendida luxu
> instruitur, mediisque parant convivia tectis:
> arte laboratae vestes ostroque superbo,
> ingens argentum mensis, caelataque in auro
> fortia facta patrum, series longissima rerum
> per tot ducta viros antiqua ab origine gentis.

The first two lines appear at the beginning of Gerald's description of the preparations ordered by Walter (289-290):

> Waltharius magnis instruxit sumptibus escas.
> luxuria in media residebat denique mensa.

Luxuria recalls Vergil's *luxu*, while *in media mensa* is an allusion to *mediisque tectis,* and *instruxit* reworks *instruitur.* The final element of the Vergilian passage, the drinking vessel embossed with representations of the heroic deeds of the host's ancestors, appears in Gerald's version after Walter's toast (308-309):

> et simul in verbo nappam dedit arte peractam
> ordine sculpturae referentem gesta priorum.

Vergil's *series longissima* is evoked by *ordine,* and of course Gerald's *gesta priorum* is an allusion to *facta priorum.* But amid the numerous verbal echoes the most important appear in the language of the toast which Walter offers his guests (304-307):

> postquam epulis depulsa fames sublataque mensa,
> heros iam dictus dominum laetanter adorsus
> inquit: «in hoc, rogito, clarescat gratia vestra,
> ut vos inprimis, reliquos tunc laetificetis.»

The first line echoes Vergil's description of the pause in the festivities (1.723: postquam prima quies epulis mensaeque remotae). The toast itself is based on Dido's words (1.731-735):

> Iuppiter, hospitibus nam te dare iura loquuntur,
> hunc laetum Tyriisque diem Troiaque profectis
> esse velis, nostrosque huius meminisse minores.
> adsit laetitiae Bacchus dator et bona Iuno;
> et vos, o coetum, Tyrii, celebrate faventes.

Gerald has worked into his passage the double occurrence of a form of *laetitia* (laetanter adorsus...laetificetis), echoing a similar double usage in the language of Dido's toast (hunc laetum...diem... / adsit laetitiae Bacchus dator). In both cases, of course, the words are meant ironically. The banquet will bring no joy to Dido; and the Huns will awaken from their boozy slumber to find Walter and Hiltgunt gone.

In Gerald's treatment of the results of the banquet we can observe an example of his ironic use of allusions to his epic models. Their feasting, as I mentioned, will bring anything but joy to Attila and the Huns. Gerald embeds two subtle hints of this fact in the narrative; for he draws on Book 9 of the *Aeneid* for two of his descriptions of the Huns' stupor. The first passage contains in fact two ominous references (318-321):

> taliter in seram produxit bachica noctem
> munera Waltharius retrahitque redire volentes,
> donec vi potus pressi somnoque gravati
> passim porticibus sternuntur humotenus omnes.

The phrase *somnoque gravati* recalls Deiphobus' use of *somnoque gravatum* (*Aeneid* 6.520) in explaining to Aeneas how he was betrayed by his wife. Moreover, the language evokes the scene in the Italian camp observed by Nisus and Euryalus when they arrive on their night foray (*Aeneid* 9.316-317: passim somno vinoque per herbam / corpora fusa vident). Later, when Gerald describes the sleeping Huns (358: populus somno vinoque solutus), the language is reminiscent of Nisus' words to describe the Rutulians (9.189: somno vinoque soluti) as he conceives the idea of a sneak attack; and no reader familiar with the *Aeneid* could fail to remember the trouble in store for them.

In this episode, the butt of Gerald's mockery is Attila. The leader of the Huns awakens with one of the few graphically described hangovers of the Latin epic tradition (362-364):

> Attila nempe manu caput amplexatus utraque
> egreditur thalamo rex Walthariumque dolendo
> advocat, ut proprium quereretur forte dolorem.

Holding his head in his hands, he is looking to share his misery on the mistaken assumption that Walter too had been drinking the night before; but he soon learns that indeed his *dolor* is worse than a mere headache. Gerald thus describes Attila's reaction to the news of Walter's escape (380-401):

> iam princeps nimia succenditur efferus ira,
> mutant laetitiam maerentia corda priorem.
> ex humeris trabeam discindit ad infima totam,
> et nunc huc animum tristem, nunc dividit illuc.
> ac velut Aeolicis turbatur arena procellis,
> sic intestinis rex fluctuat undique curis,
> et varium pectus vario simul ore imitatus
> prodidit exterius, quicquid toleraverat intus,
> iraque sermonem permisit promere nullum.
> ipso quippe die potum fastidit et escam,
> nec placidam membris potuit dare cura quietem.
> namque ubi nox rebus iam dempserat atra colores,
> decidit in lectum, verum nec lumina clausit,
> nunc latus in dextrum fultus nunc inque sinistrum,
> et veluti iaculo pectus transfixus acuto
> palpitat atque caput huc et mox iactitat illuc,

>   et modo subrectus fulcro consederat amens.
>   nec iuvat hoc, demum surgens discurrit in urbe,
>   atque thorum veniens simul attigit atque reliquit.
>   taliter insomnem consumpserat Attila noctem.
>   at profugi comites per amica silentia euntes
>   suspectam properant post terga relinquere terram.

The passage is rich in literary allusions, the effect of which is to make Attila look ridiculous (9). Gerald first recalls Walter's ironic toast by commenting that now anger (nimia succenditur efferus ira) has replaced Attila's happiness (mutant laetitiam... priorem). Attila displays that anger by ripping his royal robe. The line contains a reference to an act of grief by Aeneas (5.685: tum pius Aeneas humeris abscindere vestem), but the added touch of tearing the robe «from shoulder to bottom» seems excesive. The next line strengthens the connection with Aeneas, since it is a reminiscence of his initial confused response to Jupiter's command to leave Carthage (*Aeneid* 4.285: atque animum nunc huc celerem nunc dividit illuc). At first glance the image that follows seems also to contain a Vergilian reminiscence (ac velut Aeolicis turbatur arena procellis: storm-tossed Aeneas?); but the reference is in fact to a mocking description by Venantius Fortunatus of the digestive woes of a gluttonous abbot (non sic Aeoliis turbatur harena procellis)! Now we have a clearer notion of Gerald's purpose: Attila's grief is to elicit laughter, not sympathy. For the rest of the day he is too angry to talk and «of course» (quippe) cannot eat or drink; nor can he sleep (nec placidam membris potuit dare cura quetem). His restlessness, however, is told in language almost identical to that used by Vergil to describe Dido's *dolor* (*Aeneid* 4.5: nec placidam membris dat cura quietem) after the banquet in honor of Aeneas. At last Attila slumps into bed (decidit in lectum), and Gerald describes the time of this hardly heroic act (ubi nox rebus iam dempserat atra colores) with an

---

(9) The following discussion owes much to the sensitive analysis of this scene by Dronke, *op. cit.*

allusion to the moment when Aeneas descends into the Underworld (6.272: et rebus nox abstulit atra colorem). In this instance the juxtaposition of the action with the context of the Vergilian allusion serves to undercut the stature of Attila's wrath. Moreover, the episode concludes with a continuation of this use of Vergilian allusion to mock Attila; for the distraught pacing of the «injured» Hun (veluti iaculo pectus transfixus acuto) is reminiscent of the love-wounded Dido (4.69: qualis coniecta serva sagitta). In sum, the fearsome king of the mighty Huns is acting like a jilted, love-sick woman.

Gerald's use of a clustering of allusions to undercut the apparent seriousness of the scene depicting Attila's wrath is indicative of the ironic mood which pervades the whole epic. Mockery is, in fact, the key to Gerald's solution to the problem of making the epic a vehicle for expressing Christian values. Since previous discussions of this crucial issue have been based, for the most part, on an equation of the Christian ethos of the poem with the degree to which Walter's behavior reflects Christian values, they have failed to perceive that the *Waltharius* is at once an epic without a hero and a comic work of serious intent (10). For Gerald has taken the traditional function of epic, celebrating the excellence of a heroic individual, and inverted it to emphasize instead Walter's inadequacy as an exemplar of *virtus*. Gerald's mocking criticism of Walter is embedded in a narrative which seems to praise him, and is effected through the use of allusions to Christian literature —specifically, the Bible and Prudentius' *Psychomachia*.

The basic structural design of the *Waltharius* is founded

---

(10) Cf. the contradictory opinions of von den Steinen, *op. cit.*, p. 20: «Walter ist durchaus ein idealer Held und soll es sein: aber nicht einem klassischen Helden wie Aeneas nachgeprägt und auch nicht vom Schnitt germanischer Sagenkönige, sondern eine Gestalt, wie sie erst seit Karl dem Grossen geträumt werden konnte, bei aller Schwertgewalt christlichuntadlig und wiederum bei aller Gewissenhaftigkeit unbefangen von den kirchlichen Formen gelöst,» and of Jones, *op. cit.*, p .6: «There is evidence that Christianity is only skin-deep in the *Waltharius*. Walther asks divine forgiveness for boasting (561), yet he continues to boast thereafter without

on a successive narrowing of the focus of the narrative. It is divided into three main parts which are roughly equal in length. The first section begins with all of Europe, indeed a statement (perhaps meant to foreshadow the design of the story to come) that Europe is one of three parts of the world (1: tertia pars orbis, fratres, Europa vocatur). Then Gerald turns to the three kingdoms which send hostages to Attila. The core of the second section is Walter's fight against Gunther's men. In the final third, three warriors—Gunther, Hagen, Walter—fight among themselves. This recurrence of the number three in the design of the whole epic—three sections, three parts of the world, three warriors—provides the first hint that Gerald intends to exploit his Germanic subject matter for a Christian purpose. In this light it is of interest to note that the invocation of Gerald's prologue plays on the paradox of the oneness of God within three persons (prol. 3: personis trinus, vera deitate sed unus). Perhaps this is coincidence, perhaps another foreshadowing of the structure of the poem.

Within this basic scheme, Gerald takes care not to allow any trace of sloppy craftsmanship. He keeps track of the passage of time and, as I have discussed earlier with regard to the battle episodes, is attentive to the physical setting in which events occur (11). Occasionally he even interrupts the narrative to remind the audience of his control. Early in the tale he promises that Gunther will figure in the narrative (15: quam postea narro). Later, when he introduces the use of what may seem an anachronistic weapon, he hastens to inform us that «at that time the Franks did have arms of this sort»

---

further apology ... Even though Walther crosses himself (225) and invokes and thanks God, he shows no Christian mercy to his defenseless and imploring victims ... In other words, Christianity is not strong enough to interfere with literary tradition or secular custom.» Recently Katscher has argued for von den Steinen's position, *op. cit.*, p. 66: «Walthari verkörpert die Virtus im umfassenden Sinne und zeigt die positive Seite des Leitmotivs.»

(11) See Andersson, *op. cit.*; and Katscher, *op. cit.*, pp. 60-61.

(910: istius ergo modi Francis tunc arma fuere). At the end of the epic, when Walter, who has lost his sword, grabs a second sword called a *semispata* with his left hand, Gerald reminds us that he had already mentioned this weapon (1389-1392):

> verum vulnigeram clipeo insertaverat ulnam
> incolumique manu mox eripuit semispatam,
> qua dextram cinxisse latus memoravimus illum,
> ilico vindictam capiens ex hoste severam.

The remark to which Gerald alludes occurs more than 1000 lines earlier, as part of the description of Walter's flight from Attila (336-338):

> et laevum femur ancipiti praecinxerat ense
> atque alio dextrum pro ritu Pannoniarum:
> is tamen ex una tantum dat vulnera parte.

A sword which cuts with only one edge is a *semispata*. Amid these examples of control, I should add, there appear two seeming inconsistencies. The first concerns the cooked fish which leads to Gunther's hearing about Walter and his treasure (440-444), for it has remained fresh for a length of time that staggers the imagination; the second concerns the rather puzzling ending of the narrative. About the fish it seems fair to say that dramatic need has overcome realism; but the ending, as I will show, is by no means difficult to understand.

Since the Christian theme of the *Waltharius* is to be found in Gerald's criticism of the behavior of the main characters, I will examine in turn his characterization of Gunther, Hagen and Walter. I will begin with Gunther, in part because his utter lack of laudable qualities establishes him as a point of comparison for Gerald's more subtle attack on Hagen and Walter. In addition, the treatment of Gunther shows to good advantage the role of allusions to the *Psychomachia* in Gerald's narrative technique.

Gunther's behavior is, by any measure, unheroic. The criticism of him has three main elements. First, he is without merit as a fighter; second, he is stupid; third, he is greedy; and a final jewel in this crown of flaws is his arrogance. Walter himself offers an apt judgment of Gunther's martial prowess. After the final battle, since Gunther has shown himself sluggish (segnis) and has fought lukewarmly and without courage (qui Martis opus tepide atque enerviter egit), Walter orders Hiltgunt to serve him last of all (1413-1415):

> postremum volo Guntharius bibat, utpote segnis
> inter magnanimum qui paruit arma virorum
> et qui Martis opus tepide atque enerviter egit.

But Gunther is slow of mind as well as foot. He is described as mad (1228: demens) when he enters the fray against Walter; and he lives up to this description by coming up with a foolish (1304: ineptum) plan of attack. When the plan fails, Gunther waits «trembling and stupid» (1332: tremens stupidusque) while Hagen saves his life.

Without Gunther's greed, of course, there would be no battle at Waskenstein. When the prince learns that Walter is traveling through his domain, he thinks only of the treasure he is reputedly carrying (468-472). Gerald promises his men that Walter will surrender the treasure quickly, and later rejects Walter's offer of part of it (640-643):

> post haec Camaloni praecipit aiens:
> «perge et thesaurum reddi mihi praecipe totum.
> quodsi cunctetur—scio tu vir fortis et audax—,
> congredere et bello devictum mox spoliato.»

Nothing less than all will satisfy Gunther, even if it kills Camalo. Indeed, eleven men will die for Gunther's avarice. When Camalo's kinsman Scaramund dies, Gunther thinks mainly of the treasure (720-724). At one point the remainder of his depleted force begs Gunther to break off the battle; and the prince does appeal to vengeance rather than money (941-953). Yet here too Gerald keeps his greed before us; he calls Gunther blind (943: miser caecusque), the same word

used but a few lines earlier by Hagen to describe his nephew
(870: en caecus mortem properat gustare nefandam) as he is
goaded by his own greed to taste death.

The summation of Gunther's villainy is his *superbia*. His
arrogance and greed are, to be sure, closely connected. He is first
called arrogant (468: Guntharius princeps...superbus) when he
states for the first time his intention to wrest Walter's treasure
from him. The adjective *superbus* is next applied to Gunther
(573-574: Hagano satrapae...superbo/suggerit) when Hagen
tries unsuccessfully to dissuade his lord from sending Camalo
against Walter. I have already mentioned Gunther's call to
vengeance after the death of Scaramund (720-724):

> hunc ubi Guntharius conspexit obisse superbus,
> hortatur socios pugnam renovare furentes:
> «aggrediamur eum nec respirare sinamus,
> donec deficiens lassescat; et inde revinctus
> thesauros reddet luet et pro sanguine poenas.»

Note here again the connection between Gunther's arrogance
(Guntharius...superbus) and his greed (thesauros reddet).
More subtle is the connection between the two *vitia* in the
following passage (513-515):

> ast ubi Guntharius vestigia pulvere vidit,
> cornipedem rapidum saevis calcaribus urget,
> exultansque animis frustra sic fatur ad auras.

For these lines contain a striking allusion to the description of
Superbia herself in the *Psychomachia* (253-256):

> talia vociferans rapidum calcaribus urget
> cornipedem laxisque volat temeraria frenis
> hostem humilem cupiens inpulsu umbonis equini
> sternere deiectamque supercalcare ruinam.

Gunther urging on his horse (cornipedem rapidum saevis calca-
ribus urget) is the personification of Arrogance (rapidum calca-

ribus urget/cornipedem). A few lines later Gerald strengthens this connection. Arrogance, in her battle against Humility, is described as «unbalanced» (*Psychomachia* 203-205):

> ergo Humilem postquam male sana Superbia
> [Mentem
> vilibus instructam nullo ostentamine telis
> aspicit, in vocem dictis se effundit amaris.

Gunther too is unbalanced (530: male sana mente gravatus) —and by implication arrogant—as he presses his greedy attack against Walter.

In sum, Gunther's cowardice, dullness, greed, and arrogance place him on the opposite pole of any reasonable definition of heroic virtue. The first two qualities ill serve him in the enterprise into which he is plunged by his *avaritia* and *superbia*. Moreover, Gerald uses pointed references to the *Psychomachia* to strengthen the condemnation of Gunther as a *vir superbus*; nor does the poet let us forget that it is Gunther's obsessive desire for the treasure which Walter is carrying that precipitates the assault which results in so much death and destruction.

The negative portrait of Gunther is balanced somewhat by Gerald's description of Hagen. He is served first after the climactic battle since he is, in Walter's words, a good warrior (1411: est athleta bonus). Hagen is, in fact, Walter's equal in both strength and determination (1399-1400: duo magnanimi heroes tam viribus aequi / quam fervore animi). This comparison reiterates a statement about Walter and Hagen made at the beginning of the epic (103-105):

> qui simul ingenio crescentes mentis et aevo
> robore vincebant fortes animoque sophistas,
> donec iam cunctos superarent fortiter Hunos.

These lines reflect the conventional definition of *virtus* as a combination of wisdom (*sapientia*) and valor (*fortitudo*) (12).

---

(12) See Ernst Robert Curtius, *European Literature and the*

Both young men surpassed all the Huns—the wise in intelligence (vincebant...animoque sophistas) and the brave in strength (robore vincebant fortes). In the middle section of the narrative Hagen further displays his intelligence by trying on several occasions to dissuade Gunther from his vain quest. Among his warnings to Gunther, we should recall, is that based on the prophetic dream in which the two Franks are mutilated by a bear; but Gunther arrogantly dismisses Hagen's pessimism, accusing him falsely of mere cowardice. In further contrast to Gunther, Hagen is never described as *superbus*. He also seems to be free of *avaritia,* for he refuses an offer of treasure from Walter to desist once he has made up his mind to join the battle against his friend (1264-1279). Finally, it is Hagen whom Gerald chooses to deliver an impassioned condemnation of *avaritia* at a critical point in the tale.

Hagen's speech against greed stands at the thematic center of the *Waltharius*. It is prompted by the sight of his nephew Batavrid advancing toward an uneven fight with Walter (857-877):

> o vortex mundi, fames insatiatus habendi,
> gurges avaritiae, cunctorum fibra malorum!
> o utinam solum gluttires dira metallum
> divitiasque alias, homines impune remittens!
> sed tu nunc homines perverso numine perflans
> incendis nullique suum iam sufficit. ecce
> non trepidant mortem pro lucro incurrere turpem;
> quanto plus retinent, tanto sitis ardet habendi.
> externis modo vi modo furtive potiuntur
> et, quod plus renovat gemitus lacrimasque ciebit,
> caeligenas animas Erebi fornace retrudunt.
> ecce ego dilectum nequeo revocare nepotem,
> instimulatus enim de te est, o saeva cupido:

Latin Middle Ages, tr. Willard R. Trask (New York, 1953), pp. 174-176. The topos is found also in the Germanic heroic tradition. Beowulf, for example, is called «wise and brave» (826: snotor ond swythferhth).

> en caecus mortem properat gustare nefandam
> et vili pro laude cupit descendere ad umbras.
> heu mihi care nepos, quid matri, perdite, mandas?
> quis nuper ductam refovebit, care, maritam,
> cui nec, rapte spei, pueri ludicra dedisti?
> quis tibi nam furor est? unde haec dementia venit?
> sic ait et gremium lacrimis conspersit obortis,
> et longum «formose, vale» singultibus edit.

The harangue begins with two echoes of descriptions of Avarice by Prudentius. The phrase *fames insatiatus habendi* recalls the portrait of Avarice in the *Psychomachia* (478: amor insatiatus habendi); and the second line contains a phrase from the *Hamartigenia* (255: gurges avaritiae). Hagen's attention turns almost at once to the effect of the sin upon the behavior of men, and their willingness even to die for wealth (non trepidant mortem pro lucro incurrere turpem). The reference to death brings Hagen's thoughts back to Batavrid, who is driven by greed and a desire for fame to face Walter. Hagen's strong condemnation of greed at this moment is at once relevant and surprising. It is fitting that Gerald has chosen the beginning of a decisive battle to interrupt the narrative and have Hagen curse greed, for it is Batavrid's death that will compel him to end his obstinate refusal to join the assault against Walter. As Hagen sees his nephew stride toward his doom, he rightly deplores not only his greed but also Gunther's in sending him against Walter. On the other hand, the placement of a speech against greed at this point in the narrative is at first a surprise, since Gerald states that Batavrid was seeking not gold but glory (854: arsit enim venis laudem captare cupiscens). However, the end of the speech explains how Batavrid is in fact avaricious. Hagen continues his assertion of that greed (instimulatus enim de te est, o saeva cupido) by saying that Batavrid is blindly (en caecus) rushing to taste death (mortem properat gustare nefandam) for cheap praise (vili pro laude). Fame is thus seen as a kind of greed. Indeed, notice the repetition in this line of the language from Hagen's earlier complaint that men are willing to meet death (mortem...incurrere turpem) for wealth (pro lucro).

By condemning Batavrid for greed when the young man is seeking fame, Hagen's speech accomplishes two things. First, it makes explicit the nature of Gerald's criticism of the Germanic heroic code as founded on *avaritia*: the desire for treasure is a self-evident kind of avarice, and now the warrior's concern for fame is revealed also as greed. Second, this equation of glory with greed provides the basis for a later condemnation of Hagen's own behavior. He is drawn into the final assault on Walter only to avenge the death of his nephew. When he confronts Walter, he gives the following explanation for his decision (1275-1279):

> haec res est, pactum quia irritasti prior almum,
> iccircoque gazam cupio pro foedere nullam.
> sitne tibi soli virtus, volo discere in armis,
> deque tuis manibus caedem perquiro nepotis.
> en aut oppeto sive aliquid memorabile faxo.

Two elements of this speech stand out. First, Hagen states clearly that he is motivated by a desire for revenge (deque tuis manibus caedem perquiro nepotis). Second, although he disclaims any interest in the treasure (gazam cupio...nullam), he does express a concern about glory (aliquid memorabile faxo). In doing so, Hagen involves himself with the taint of *avaritia* as a result of his own earlier equation of the desire for glory with that sin.

We can see, then, that Gerald uses Hagen's speech against avarice to underscore the importance of that theme in the *Waltharius*. The long complaint is delivered at a critical moment, just as Batavrid leaves for the fight which will result in Hagen's entering the fray. It is used to criticize the two motives of the Germanic warrior—wealth and fame. Although Hagen is speaking specifically about his nephew, by implication he is criticizing Gunther as well; and I have shown that by linking the desire for fame with greed Hagen sets the stage for his own admission of avarice in his speech to Walter. Finally, it should be noted that none of the killing would have occurred had Walter not taken the treasure with him in the first place.

We turn now to Walter. He is the central figure of the epic, as Gerald informs us in the prologue (prol. 17-18: resonat sed mira tyronis / nomine Waltharius) and in the last line of the narrative (1456: haec est Waltharii poesis). The final narrowing of the focus of the story directs our attention to him alone, with a comment on his thirty years of happy rule in Aquitaine. Are then Gunther and Hagen, not to mention Attila, his foils, lesser characters whose function is to cast Walter's heroic excellence in sharper relief? I think not: for a careful reading will reveal that Walter is no more an idealized Christian hero than is Hagen or Gunther, and that while by classical or Germanic standards Walter may seem admirable, when judged by Christian standards he is not.

Much about Walter's character is, to be sure, praiseworthy. The first section of the narrative, in particular, stresses his noble qualities. We have seen already that Walter, along with Hagen, surpassed all others at Attila's court in *sapientia* and *fortitudo*. The escape of Hagen removes him temporarily from the story and allows Gerald to concentrate on offering illustrations of these two qualities in Walter's behavior. Indeed, with Hagen gone, Attila's wife urges her husband to keep Walter, the prop of his empire (126: vestri imperii...columna), at court by convincing him to marry; but Walter, who is already contemplating his own escape (144: iam tum praemeditans, quod post compleverat actis), foils this plan. The next scene illustrates his martial valor. Not only does he plan the campaign against the rebel tribe (173: tunc ad Waltharium convertitur actio rerum) but he also promises to fight with his usual valor (177: solita virtute). There is, I should add, a potential for irony in the phrase, which is borowed from the description of herself by Patiens in the *Psychomachia* (156). What follows immediately, however, is Walter's *aristeia* (196-200) as a demonstration of his *fortitudo*. After stressing Walter's bravery, Gerald returns to his intelligence, for the next scene concerns the plan of the *vir sapiens* (240) which will enable him and Hiltgunt to escape. When they are gone, Attila's wife repeats her description of Walter as *imperii columna* (376), while the king of the Huns, despite offering the powerful inducements of gold and glory (411-412: laudem captare perennem / ...gazam infarcire cruminis), can find no warriors to pursue Walter. They are all just too aware of his valor (415: nota equidem virtus).

In addition to *fortitudo* and *sapientia,* the first section of the narrative also introduces the flaw which will provide the foundation for Gerald's mocking condemnation of Walter. When he explains the escape plan to Hiltgunt, he quite understandably instructs her first to get armor (261-265); but his thoughts then turn at once to gold (265-267):

> ...bina dehinc mediocria scrinia tolle.
> his armillarum tantum da Pannonicarum,
> donec vix unum releves ad pectoris imum.

Only after telling Hiltgunt to load two boxes so heavily that she can hardly lift them does Walter think of such necessities as shoes and fish hooks. Gerald, moreover, reminds us of the treasure when the two former hostages set out on their westward journey (326-330). Indeed, it is fair to say that from this point until almost the conclusion of the epic the treasure occupies center stage: Gunther wants it, and Walter fights to keep it.

In the central portion of the narrative, the treasure seems to define for Walter his view of right action. At the first sight of the approaching band of Franks, Hiltgunt, mistaking them for Huns, immediately asks Walter to kill her and spare her from having to «suffer sexual contact» (547: patiar consortia carnis) with any other man. After comforting her, Walter recognizes the insignia of the Franks, but thinks immediately of his treasure (561-563):

> hac coram porta verbum modo iacto superbum:
> hinc nullus rediens uxori dicere Francus
> praesumet se impune gazae quid tollere tantae.

He has not yet been attacked or even addressed by any of the Franks; nevertheless, Walter is already suspicious of their motives concerning his gold. The reference to the wives of the Franks does remind Walter of Hiltgunt, and the expresses his hope to be preserved for her out of the expected battle (571: ex pugna tibi, Hiltgunt sponsa, reservor). But at the heart of his boast is the system of values of the Germanic heroic code: Walter cares about his reputation (nullus...uxori dicere Francus / praesumet) and his possessions (gazae quid tollere tantae). He will fight, in sum, to keep his treasure and to avoid the shame of losing it.

Reputation and revenge are recurring themes in the description of Walter's struggle against Gunther's retainers. When Camalo is killed, his nephew Scaramund demands the right to attack next in order to avenge his kinsman (691: carum ulciscar amicum). The fifth warrior, Hadaward, vows that he will compel Walter to suffer punishment for his crimes (820: tum demum scelerum cruciamina pendes). He is followed by Batavrid, who fights for fame and not vengeance (854: laudem captare cupiscens); but his death motivates first Gerwit (914: hunc sese ulturum spondens Gerwitus adivit) and later, as we saw, Hagen. By the time the eighth vassal, Randolf by name, attacks him, Walter too is acting as much out of a concern for his reputation as out of a desire to keep what he considers to be his rightful property. When Randolf cuts off some of Walter's hair, the exhausted warrior is enraged (979-981):

> «en pro calvitio capitis te vertice fraudo,
> ne fiat ista tuae de me iactantia sponsae.»
> vix effatus haec truncavit colla precantis.

Walter decapitates Randolf, though he begs for mercy (haec truncavit colla precantis), to prevent the Frank from boasting even that he gave Walter a bald spot! To the last Frank to die in this series of combats Walter again speaks of vengeance (1056-1059):

>   ...exin
> Alpharides: «morere» inquit «et haec sub Tartara
>   [transfer
> enarrans sociis, quod tu sis ultus eosdem.»
> his dictis torquem collo circumdedit aureum.

Walter slits the man's throat (for that is the meaning of the «bright necklace» he gives him) and sends the Frank to inform his dead companions of his failure to avenge them. Finally, the transition from this section of the narrative to its final third turns on Gunther's appeal to Hagen on the basis of the Franks' irreparable loss of reputation (1085: dedecus at tantum superabit Francia numquam) if Walter should escape unharmed (1088: impune).

An awesome warrior who to protect a treasure has just killed eleven men, four of whom he decapitated, is an unlikely exemplar of Christian virtue, especially in a work addressed to monks; however, since Walter has been interpreted more than once as the embodiment of a new «Christian» concept of heroic virtue, it is necessary to examine those acts of his which might support such a reading of the text. The notion that Walter's actions reflect Christian values, to be sure rests upon slim evidence. The first indication that he is in fact a Christian man occurs when he makes the sign of the cross (225: qui signans accipiebat) before drinking a beaker of wine. Later, while fleeing with Hiltgunt from the Huns, Walter refrains from sexual intercourse with his beautiful betrothed (cf. 456-457: incredibili formae decorata nitore / ...puella), and for his continence earns Gerald's praise (427: laudabilis heros). Of considerably more significance, however, are two events which frame the middle portion of the narrative. Just before the attacks by Gunther's men begin, Walter vows, as we saw, to protect his name and his treasure (561-563); however, he sudenly interrupts this expression of a proud boast (561: verbum modo iacto superbum) and repents for having said such a thing (564-565):

> necdum sermonem complevit, humotenus ecce
> corruit et veniam petit, quia talia dixit.

This expression of humility is assuredly out of character for a pagan hero; and it is in striking contrast to the attitude of Walter's antagonist Gunther, who not much before was described as a personification of Superbia (513-515). Moreover, contrition and prayer mark Walter's behavior at the end of the combats against Gunther's men as well (1150-1167):

> his ita provisis exploratisque profatur:
> «en quocumque modo res pergant, hic recubabo,
> donec circuiens lumen spera reddat amatum,
> ne patriae fines dicat rex ille superbus
> evasisse fuga furis de more per umbas.»
> dixit et ecce viam vallo praemuniit artam
> undique praecisis spinis simul et paliuris.
> quo facto ad truncos sese convertit amaro
> cum gemitu et cuicumque suum caput applicat atque
> contra orientalem prostratus corpore partem
> ac nudum retinens ensem hac voce precatur:
> «rerum factori, sed et omnia facta regenti,
> nil sine permisso cuius vel denique iusso
> constat, ago grates, quod me defendit iniquis
> hostilis turmae telis nec non quoque probris.
> deprecor at dominum contrita mente benignum,
> ut qui peccantes non vult sed perdere culpas,
> hos in caelesti praestet mihi sede videri.»

While still concerned about his reputation, in that he will not slip away from Gunther «like a thief» (furis de more), Walter is also strongly moved by feelings of remorse. After searching out the trunks of the four men whom he has decapitated, Walter joins their severed heads to their bodies (cuicumque suum caput applicat). His prayer, though thanking God for preserving him from a loss of reputation (nec non quoque probris), also expresses the hope of meeting his attackers in heaven (hos in caelesti praestet mihi sede videri). This prayer, made in a spirit of contrition (contrita mente) contains the expression of an idea which is central to Gerald's treatment of the *avaritia* theme; for Walter's prayer on behalf of his enemies is based on the belief that God wishes to destroy sins, not sinners (qui peccantes non vult sed perdere culpas).

This last episode is commonly cited as proof that Walter is a new kind of hero who joins compassion to the traditional qualities of valor and intelligence; however, a closer examination casts doubt on this view; for it must be admitted that Walter's compassion, like his rather macabre acts of kindness, comes too late. The men are, after all, dead; nor are these feelings of compassion as strong as the more conventional attitudes of a warrior. On the following morning, Walter goes out and despoils those same dead (1191-1197):

> aggreditur iuvenis caesos spoliarier armis
> armorumque habitu, tunicas et cetera linquens:
> armillas tantum, cum bullis baltea et enses,
> loricas quoque cum galeis detraxerat ollis.
> quatuor his oneravit equos sponsamque vocatam
> imposuit quinto, sextum conscenderat ipse
> et primus vallo perrexerat ipse revulso.

The picture of Walter and Hiltgunt departing with a horse—or rather horses, since the two in this case have more treasure and get a chance to ride themselves—laden with treasure recalls their flight from Attila. Even the language of the latter scene (armillas tantum) calls attention to the arm-rings (266: armillarum tantum) taken from the Huns. The passage contains also an allusion to the *Aeneid,* to Euryalus' despoiling of the Rutulians (9.357-363), thus reminding us that Walter is behaving in accord with the pagan heroic tradition rather than a Christian attitude of compassion. Walter's own words reflect this almost immediate return to a non-Christian morality. Thus he speaks when he realizes that Hagen and Gunther have lured him from his stronghold only to attack him together (1215-1218):

> incassum multos mea dextera fuderat hostes,
> si modo supremis laus desit, dedecus assit.
> est satius pulcram per vulnera quaerere mortem
> quam solum amissis palando evadere rebus.

By his own admission Walter is fighting in order that his right hand may not have slain many enemies in vain (incassum multos mea dextera fuderat hostes). He fears the absence of glory and the presence of ill fame (laus desit, dedecus assit) which will occur if he escapes without his possessions (solum amissis palando evadere rebus). God is not mentioned.

The sequence of events described above is typical of Gerald's undercutting of any possible interpretation of Walter as steadfastly Christian in his attitude or behavior. For another example, his rejection of boasting is soon forgotten (561-565) when he chides a warrior before killing him (750-753) and sends another to the Underworld with a message from Walter boasting of victory (1056-1058); nor is Walter's concern with the accomplishments of his right hand (multos mea dextera fuderat hostes) an isolated moment. Before killing Hadaward, Walter addresses both his hands (812-817):

> viribus o summis hostem depellere cures,
> dextera, ne rapiat tibi propugnacula muri!
> tu clavum umbonis studeas retinere, sinistra,
> atque ebori digitos circumfer glutine fixos!
> istic ne ponas pondus, quod tanta viarum
> portasti spatia, ex Avarum nam sedibus altis!

Their function is to repel the enemy (hostem repellere) and thus to avoid the loss of the treasure (ne ponas pondus) which has been transported so great a distance. Most interesting, however, is Walter's address to Hiltgunt earlier in the story when she believes that the Huns have found them (548-553):

> tum iuvenis: «cruor innocuus me tinxerit?» inquit
> et: «quo forte modo gladius potis est inimicos
> sternere, tam fidae si nunc non parcit amicae?

> absit quod rogitas, mentis depone pavorem.
> qui me de variis eduxit saepe periclis,
> hic valet hic hostes, credo, confundere nostros.

In whom—or what—is Walter placing his trust? One's first impression is to say God, especially given the evocation of the Bible in Walter's words (2 Cor. 1.10: qui de tantis periculis nos eripuit). On the other hand, the antecedent of *qui* in this passage grammatically could well be the sword (gladius potis est inimicos sternere) to which Walter has just referred. The wording of the statement allows either God or Walter's sword to be the *hic* which can confound his enemies; for we have here, I suggest, an example of the studied ambiguity which Sedulius employs so effectively in the *De Quodam Verbece*. If Walter means God, then he will contradict this assertion by those later expressions of faith in his right hand which I have already cited (812-817, 1215-1218). That he is more likely to mean his sword may be indicated by the fact that the simile of the bear which Gerald uses to describe Walter is based, as I showed, on a simile used by Vergil to describe Mezentius; for in the same episode Mezentius invokes his right hand as his god (*Aeneid* 10. 773-774: dextra mihi deus et telum.../nunc adsint!). However, if Walter does mean his sword, then like Mezentius' his confidence is ill founded. Of one of Gunther's men whom Walter soon will kill Gerald says that he vainly trusted in his sword alone (784: in solum confisus inaniter ensem). The reference is to the man's foolishness in leaving his spear behind; but I think that the criticism can be applied figuratively also to Walter, who but a few lines afterward will address his two hands (812-817) but leave God behind.

In sum, Walter's avarice prevents him from being a model of Christian virtue. Once he has taken the treasure from the Huns, he is preoccupied both with keeping it and with avoiding the shame of losing it. As with Attila's warriors, the two motives which prod Walter into action are the desire for reputation and for wealth. During the fighting he places his trust in his sword-bearing right hand rather tham in God. In the heat of battle his «Christian» feelings of compassion and remorse melt away, leaving a core of values which bear little resemblance to an idealized Christian ethic.

Walter's outlook, however, is not to be confused with the outlook of the *Waltharius*. As I suggested earlier, the Christian theme of the epic is to be found in Gerald's criticism of his cast of «heroic» characters. The poet draws together the disparate threads of the narrative in a brilliantly conceived final scene which makes its mocking point through direct moralizing, a clustering of allusions to the *Psychomachia,* and an apparent act of carelessness on the part of the poet which in fact is meant to draw our attention to a Biblical quotation that provides the key to the underlying meaning of the narrative.

The ending of the *Waltharius* has been regarded as a puzzle (13). If so, it is not by accident that it is puzzling; for in the narrative Gerald gives clear indication of the importance of the outcome of the climactic battle pitting Walter alone against Gunther and Hagen. The sequence of events of that battle is briefly as follows. When Walter, attempting to escape, is overtaken by his two adversaries, he offers Hagen gifts to dissuade him from breaking their long-standing friendship. The latter, however, declares that pact already broken and demands repayment for the death of Batavrid. In the ensuing struggle, each man is grievously wounded. Walter cuts off Gunther's leg above the knee; but before he can finish off the prince, Hagen jumps in his way. When Walter's sword shatters on Hagen's helmet, the angry and frustrated Walter throws away the useless hilt. Hagen takes this opportunity to slice off Walter's outstretched right hand. With his left

---

(13) Von den Steinen, *op. cit.,* p. 19, explains away the ending by saying that it shows the poet was dealing with traditional material which he could not alter even though it made little sense. Jones, *op. cit.,* p. 18, speaks of the «trick ending» of the narrative. The puzzling nature of the conclusion is perhaps best reflected in the number of critics who simply ignore the problems which it poses for their reading of the poem.

hand, however, Walter grabs a one-edged sword and puts out Hagen's right eye as well as six of his teeth. The three men, injured and exhausted, now lay down their weapons. Walter orders Hiltgunt to serve wine, after which the men enjoy some rather cruel jokes about their wounds, and then go their separate ways. Gerald mentions that Walter will reach home, marry Hiltgunt, and rule happily in Aquitaine for thirty years.

The first two thirds of the epic contain several foreshadowings of this conclusion. Through the device of Hagen's dream, Gerald informs us in advance of the wounds to be suffered by Gunther and Hagen. He also uses the simile of the bear to recall that prophecy less than fifty lines before describing the event itself. The injury to Walter calls to mind not only that warrior's earlier imprecation to his right hand but also his reference to that hand at the beginning of the episode. Moreover, the second section of the narrative ends with a battle (1021-1061) which has much in common with the final combat. Here too Walter fights alone against two men—in this case Trogus and Tanastus. Walter cuts off the right hand of Trogus (1045: et cursu advolitans dextram ferientis ademit); but a second blow designed to finish off the injured foe lands instead on the interposed shield of Tanastus. Walter is angered (1050: hinc indignatus iram convertit in ipsum) and wrenches Tanastus' shoulder from its socket before killing him. He then returns to his interrupted business with Trogus. Although the outcome is different—neither Trogus nor Tanastus being, after all, of Hagen's might—we can see acted out here two basic events of the final combat: the amputation of a right hand and Walter's frustration when his sword blow is thwarted by a second warrior. Added to the information contained in Hagen's dream, this episode provides us with foreknowledge of what will happen to all three combattants in the final struggle.

The two key elements of the final scene are the wounds which the men inflict on one another and the sudden halt to the fighting. The wounds unquestionably have symbolic meaning. Consider the most obvious example. Hagen loses an eye and six teeth. And what is his expressed motivation for joining at last the assault against Walter? Revenge. Surely no monk would have missed the appropriateness of these wounds or the evocation of the Biblical injunction «an eye for an eye, a tooth for a tooth» (Exodus 21:22-25).

Gerald even intrudes into the narrative in order to emphasize the importance of the set of wounds and relate them to his moral stance (1401-1404):

> postquam finis adest, insignia quemque notabant:
> illic Guntharii regis pes, palma iacebat
> Waltharii nec non tremulus Haganonis ocellus.
> sic sic armillas partiti Avarenses!

Not only the vividness of this gruesome list—Hagen's eye is still twitching (nec non tremulus)!—but also the exclamation with its repetition of *sic* call attention to the importance of the information. And yet the list is inaccurate. It fails to make mention of Hagen's missing teeth; moreover, although Walter had hacked off Gunther's whole leg including the knee up to the thigh (1369: crus cum poplite adusque femur), the catalogue mentions only the amputated foot. These seeming errors are most unusual lapses on the part of a poet who, as I have shown, prides himself on attention to accuracy in even minor details. But they are not lapses. The omission and change serve to turn the catalogue of wounds into another unmistakable scriptural reference (Mark 9.42-48):

> And if your hand causes you to sin, cut it off; it is better for you to enter life maimed than with two hands to go to hell, to the unquenchable fire. And if your foot causes you to sin, cut it off; it is better for you to enter life lame than with two feet to be thrown into hell. And if your eye causes you to sin, pluck it out; it is better for you to enter the kingdom of God with one eye than with two eyes to be thrown into hell, where the worm does not die, and the fire is not quenched.

Gerald's use of this allusion provides the key to unlocking the meaning beneath the lively surface narrative. The obvious implication is that the wounds are meant to be viewed as punishments suffered by the three men for yielding to temptation. Walter, by taking the treasure, and Gunther, by pursuing it, have yielded directly to avarice. Hagen has yielded indirectly by giving in to his desire for vengeance and then declaring his concern for glory.

Since Walter is the central character of the epic, the symbolism of the injury inflicted on him is developed more fully. His wound calls to mind a corresponding passage in Matthew which refers to the cutting off of one's *right* hand (Matthew 5.30):

> And if your right hand causes you to sin, cut it off and throw it away; it is better that you lose one of your members than that your whole body go into hell.

When we remember Walter's earlier avowed faith in his right hand to protect his possessions, the loss of that hand seems singularly appropriate. But Gerald establishes an even more precise connection between Walter's wound and punishment for his greed. To understand fully that connection, we must now turn our attention back to the *Psychomachia*.

Allusions to the *Psychomachia* play an important role in Gerald's description of the events leading up to and including the thoughtless act which renders Walter vulnerable to Hagen's attack (1333-1385). The scene is designed to emphasize that Walter's outlook is essentially unChristian. The bear simile (1337-1345) at the beginning of the scene links him to the pagan Mezentius. Next, Gerald allows Walter to reveal in his own words that his outlook as a warrior is pagan rather than Christian. I mentioned earlier that the rest of the narrative casts doubt on the assumption that Walter trusts in God to protect him. If Walter does forget God when striving to keep his treasure, what force does he see operating in human affairs? When he begins to lose heart, the following thought steals into his mind (1347-1349):

> interea herois coepit subrepere menti
> quiddam, qui tacito premit has sub corde loquelas:
> «si Fortuna viam non commutaverit, isti
> vana fatigatum memet per ludicra fallent.»

Walter expresses his fear that Hagen and Gunther will trick him, tired as he is (fatigatum memet per ludicra fallent). But it is Fortuna not God in whom he sees the power to change things (si Fortuna viam non commutaverit). Though he is like Gunther in mercifully few respects, Walter seems to share his attitude at least concerning the power of Fortuna; for earlier the mad king (1228: rex...demens), imagining that even supernatural forces share his own failings, had accused Walter of having bribed Fortuna (1236: scio, Fortunam mercede vocasti). And it is especially important to note that Walter's reference to Fortuna at this point in the battle is reminiscent of the complaint of Avaritia in the *Psychomachia* that Fortuna is mocking her vain efforts (525: et cassos ludit Fortuna lacertos).

Walter's concern, like that expressed by Avaritia, that his efforts have been in vain surfaces in his next speech, a taunting challenge to Hagen to stand and fight (1350-1355):

> ilico et elata Haganoni voce profatur:
> «o paliure, vires foliis, ut pungere possis;
> tu saltando iocans astu me ludere temptas.
> sed iam faxo locum, propius ne accedere tardes:
> ecce tuas—scio, praegrandes—ostendito vires!
> me piget incassum tantos sufferre labores.»

In addition to a pun on Hagen's name (paliure = hagen-dorn) and a verbal allusion to the bear simile (propius...accedere), this passage contains in its last line an instructive double reminiscence within the *Waltharius* and to the *Aeneid*. The internal reference is to Walter's earlier boast that he will not allow his right hand to have slain so many men in vain (1215: incassum)—an allusion which also recalls Avaritia's statement concerning Fortuna. The Vergilian reminiscence reestablishes the link between Walter and Turnus which I demonstrated in my analysis of the middle section of the epic. For when Walter declares that he is tired of undergoing so many labors in vain (me piget incassum tantos sufferre labores), he repeats almost exactly the words addressed to Turnus by Allecto (*Aeneid* 7.421: Turne, tot incassum fusos patiere labores) when that dire fiend arouses him to anger (7.445: talibus Allecto dictis exarsit in iras).

Walter's own anger and its baleful consequences are the subject of the rest of the scene. He cuts off Gunther's leg, but loses his temper when his sword breaks on Hagen's helmet (1371-1385):

>extensam cohibere manum non quiverat heros,
>sed cassis fabrefacta diu meliusque peracta
>excipit assultum mox et scintillat in altum.
>cuius duritia stupefactus dissilit ensis,
>proh dolor! et crepitans partim micat aere et herbis.
>belliger ut frameae murcatae fragmina vidit,
>indigne tulit ac nimia furit efferus ira
>impatiensque sui capulum sine pondere ferri,
>quamlibet eximio praestaret et arte metallo,
>protinus abiecit monimentaque tristia sprevit.
>qui dum forte manum iam enormiter exeruisset,
>abstulit hanc Hagano sat laetus vulnere prompto.
>in medio iactus recidebat dextera fortis
>gentibus ac populis multis suspecta, tyrannis,
>innumerabilibus quae fulserat ante trophaeis.

In this passage too we can observe the skilful intertwining of allusions to both the *Aeneid* and the *Psychomachia*. On the one hand, the purpose of the connection between Walter and Turnus is made clear. Walter raises his sword (spatam tollens) for the death blow; but when Hagen's helmet receives the blow (obiecit ad ictum), the sword shatters (dissilit ensis) and the pieces glitter in the grass (partim micat...herbis). So it is also with Turnus when at last he faces Aeneas. He puts his all into one sword stroke (*Aeneid* 12.729: alte sublatum consurgit Turnus in ensem); but in the middle of the blow

(12.732: in medio...ictu) the blade shatters (12.740-741: mortalis mucro...ictu / dissiluit) and the fragments glitter in the sand (12.741: fulva resplendent fragmina harena). Turnus is to die; and Gerald, by this series of allusions, provides still another foreshadowing of *dolor* in store for Walter.

The shattering of Walter's sword contains as well an important clustering of verbal references to the *Psychomachia*. In like maner the sword of Ira shatters against the well wrought helmet of Patiens (132-144). The similarities between the two passages are closest in their description of the reactions of the disappointed warriors. Consider Ira (145-150):

> ira, ubi truncati mucronis fragmina vidit
> et procul in partes ensem crepuisse minutas,
> iam capulum retinente manu sine pondere ferri,
> mentis inops ebur infelix decorisque pudendi
> perfida signa abicit monumentaque tristia longe
> spernit, et ad proprium succenditur effera letum.

When she sees the broken fragments (truncati mucronis fragmina vidit) and the useless hilt (capulum...sine pondere ferri), she throws away the wretched reminder (abicit monumentaque tristia / longe spernit) and rages uncontrollably (succenditur effera). And now Walter: Angered (nimia furit efferus ira) when he sees his shattered sword (frameae murcatae fragmina vidit) and useless hilt (sui capulum sine pondere ferri), Walter disdainfully throws away the unwelcome reminder (protinus abiecit monimenta tristia sprevit). Yet the number of pointed allusions in this passage is still not exhausted. Now Walter is *impatiens*—quite a change for the man who earlier (177) had described himself in language recalling Ira's foe Patientia. Moreover, in picturing the angry Walter as *nimia...efferus ira* Gerald uses the same phrase which is applied to Attila when he realizes Walter has escaped (380: nimia succenditur efferus ira); and Attila's anger, we recall, was ridiculed by Gerald through the comparison of the Hun with Dido. Given this complex of references, then, to the *Aeneid* and *Psychomachia*, we might say that Walter gets off lightly. Turnus dies by the sword of Aeneas, and Ira is so maddened that she kills herself. But Walter's action causes him to lose «only» his right hand. And Gerald concludes the scene by lingering over a description of that severed hand lying on the ground (1383-1385), thus prefiguring its presence (1401: palma iacebat) in the catalogue of wounds a few lines later.

In the episode which I have just examined, Gerald's use of allusions to the *Psychomachia* to connect Walter with the figure of Ira is one of several devices by which he casts his hero's behavior in a negative light. More important, however, are the allusions in this episode and the next (the cessation of hostilities) to Prudentius' description of Avaritia, the Sin who is perhaps the most dangerous of the seven striving with the Virtues for control of the human soul. The allusions to her in this episode are drawn mainly from Prudentius' account of her entrance onto the field of battle (454-463):

> fertur Avaritia gremio praecincta capaci,
> quidquid Luxus edax pretiosum liquerat, unca
> corripuisse manu, pulchra in ludibria vasto
> ore inhians aurique legens fragmenta caduci
> inter harenarum cumulos. nec sufficit amplos
> implevisse sinus; iuvat infercire cruminis
> turpe lucrum et gravidos furtis distendere fiscos,
> quos laeva celante tegit laterisque sinistri
> velat opermento; velox nam dextra rapinas
> abradit spoliisque ungues exercet aenos.

Gerald has already made reference to this description of Greed. When Attila is exhorting his men to pursue Walter, noone is willing despite the desire to win glory and «cram treasure in money-bags» (412: gazam infarcire cruminis). There the allusion to Avaritia cramming her base gain in money-bags (iuvat infercire cruminis / turpe lucrum) clearly reflects a criticism of the usual motives of Germanic warriors—an attack which is developed more fully in Hagen's long speech before the death of Batavrid. The rest of Prudentius' picture, especially the image of Avaritia scraping up spoils (rapinas /

abradit) with her swift right hand (velox nam dextra) is most effective. Perhaps the notion of scraping inspired the sword that that scraped off some of Walter's hair (971-972: vertice crines / abrasit) but was not able to graze his scalp (972: cutem praestringere summam); in the *Psychomachia* the weapons hurled by Greed likewise inflict only superficial cuts (506-507: vix in cute summa / praestringens). But the most relevant feature of Prudentius' description is the picture of Avaritia grabbing after plunder with her right hand; hence, it is proper, indeed inevitable, that Walter lose the grasping right hand that he depended on to protect the plunder which his avarice led him to have stuffed into treasure chests.

We turn now to the warriors' sudden cessation of hostilities. In this instance too Gerald is employing imitation of the *Psychomachia* to underscore the criticism of avarice as the Christian message of his epic. In Prudentius' narrative, after Avaritia has been killed, victorious Operatio announces that now is the time for the Virtues to rest and refresh themselves (606-608):

solvite procinctum, iusti, et discedite ab armis!
causa mali tanti iacet interfecta; lucrandi
ingluvie pereunte licet requiescere sanctis.

This episode (603-663) in the *Psychomachia* provides the model for the drinking which ends the *Waltharius*. The cause for rejoicing among the Virtues is the defeat of Avaritia (causa mali tanti iacet interfecta). Rest is possible only after the lust for gain is dead (lucrandi / ingluvie pereunte). Operatio's next words describe the true rest of those without greed (609-628). Among her exhortations to moderation is one which has special significance for the reader of the *Waltharius*; for she advises her colleagues when setting out on a journey not even to carry a wallet (613: ingressurus iter peram ne tollito) but to trust in God to provide for their needs. How different was Walter's attitude in taking so much treasure when he fled Attila! From Gerald's Christian viewpoint, that deed is avarice; and the rest enjoyed by the three warriors is like that of the Virtues after the death of Avaritia. In this case, the sin has been, if not defeated, at least amply punished.

Finally, what are we to make of the crude banter which follows (1421-1442):

> hic tandem Hagano spinosus et ipse Aquitanus,
> mentibus invicti, licet omni corpore lassi,
> post varios pugnae strepitus ictusque tremendos
> inter pocula scurrili certamine ludunt.
> Francus ait: «iam dehinc servos agitabis, amice,
> quorum de corio wantis sine fine fruaris:
> et dextrum, moneo, tenera lanugine comple,
> ut causae ignaros palmae sub imagine fallas.
> wah! sed quid dicis, quod ritum infringere gentis
> ac dextro femori gladium agglomerare videris
> uxorique tuae, si quando ea cura subintrat,
> perverso amplexu circumdabis euge sinistram?
> iam quid demoror? en posthac tibi quicquid
> [agendum est,
> laeva manus faciet.» cui Walthare talia reddit:
> «cur tam prosilias, admiror, lusce Sicamber:
> si venor cervos, carnem vitabis aprinam.
> ex hoc iam famulis tu suspectando iubebis
> heroum turbas transversa tuendo salutans.
> sed fidei memor antiquae tibi consiliabor:
> iam si quando domum venias laribusque propinques,
> effice lardatam de multra farreque pultam:
> haec pariter victum tibi conferet atque medelam.

Such a flitting would be customary among Germanic warriors. But the content of the jokes is what matters here. Hagen tells Walter he will henceforth need to fill one of his gloves with down to fool people into believing that he has two hands; but from now on he has only his left hand for holding his sword or his wife—or doing anything at all. Walter replies with jibes at Hagen's future life of soft food and sidelong glances. Moreover, after the two are finished, they have to lift up the severely injured Gunther (1444: regem tollentes valde dolentem) and put him on his horse. Then Gerald, to say that they go their separate ways (1445: sic disiecti redierunt), uses the word *disiecti*. It can mean «in different directions;» it can also mean «torn to pieces.» For at the end of his epic Gerald still wants our attention on the wounds suffered by the three «heroes»; and in this context we need not wonder why he seems to forget about the treasure which has been central to the narrative for so long. It has served his purpose; for Gerald has revealed that the warrior's preoccupation with wealth as a material symbol of his worth is by Christian standards a form of greed. The wounds inflicted on Walter, Hagen, and Gunther are punishment enough for their actions; for as Walter himself says, more aptly than he knows, God wishes to destroy not sinners but sins (1166: peccantes non vult sed perdere culpas).

The conclusion of the *Waltharius* is in no way inconsistent with the rest of the narrative. It may seem odd at first that Walter and his two foes so quickly give up the fighting, and that Gerald makes no further mention of the *armillae Avarenses* for which they were contending with such bitterness. However, these apparent inconsistencies, like that in the catalogue of wounds, are dissolved once we perceive them as elements of Gerald's larger theme, the mockery of the *avaritia* which prevents Walter or any of the others from being a model of Christian heroism. Each inconsistency in fact directs us to a sub-text: the list of wounds to the Bible, and the sudden end of the combat to the *Psychomachia*. Both the overall design of the *Waltharius* and Gerald's use of foreshadowing emphasize the importance of the conclusion, which in turn makes explicit the ironic intent of what has gone before. Gerald, while utilizing the trappings of epic, has turned the genre to a new purpose. He resolves the problem of welding Christian content to a Germanic story told in classical form by attacking the values of at first glance heroic figures and rendering them ridiculous. In his prologue, Gerald speaks of the *Waltharius* as an entertainment (prol. 19: ludendum est), and we have seen that his epic indeed is filled with mocking humor. But we should not forget that sin is the butt of that humor, and in the ridicule of misplaced values lies the poem's Christian spirit.

MOCKING HEROISM:
ALEXANDER THE GREAT AND THE PURSUIT
OF GLORY

> The story of Alisaundre is so commune,
> That every wight that hath discrecioun
> Hath heard somewhat or all of his fortune.
> *The Monks Tale* 641-643.
>
> Alexander died, Alexander was buried,
> Alexander returneth into dust; the dust is
> earth; of earth we make loam; and why of
> that loam, whereto he was converted, might
> they not stop a beer-barrel?
> *Hamlet,* Act V, Scene 1

Walter of Châtillon had already established his reputation as a writer of importance when, in 1176, he began an epic poem on the career of Alexander the Great. We know little for certain about Walter's life (1). We do know that he was born *ca.* 1135, that he studied for a time at Paris, and that shortly thereafter he became head of the school at Laon, a position he gave up to be a canon at Reims. In the 1160s Walter joined the chancery of Henry II of England, where he became a friend of John of Salisbury. Early in the 1170's, disenchanted with Henry, Walter left England and became a teacher in Châtillon (probably Châtillon-sur-Marne). It was

---

(1) For the sources of information concerning Walter's life see Max Manitius, *Geschichte der lateinischen Literatur des Mittelalters* III (Munich, 1931), pp. 920-936. Consult also Heinrich Christensen, *Das Alexanderlied Walters von Châtillon* (Halle a. S., 1905), pp. 1-76.

during this period that his production of shorter poems, as now represented in the St. Omer MS and Strecker's collection of *moralisch-satirische Gedichte*, brought Walter fame and linked his name henceforth with Châtillon (2). In 1176 William of Champagne, who was then Archbishop of Sens, exchanged his diocese for that of Reims. When he arrived there, he appointed Walter as his notary and public orator. It was to his patron William that the *Alexandreis* was dedicated by Walter.

The *Alexandreis* secured Walter's position as one of the most accomplished poets of the twelfth century; and not coincidentally it earned him the reward of being made a canon at Amiens. The existence today of more than 200 manuscripts of the epic, many written within a century of its composition, attests to the immediate and continued popularity of Walter's narrative. In the thirteenth century, in fact, the *Alexandreis* was used as a textbook in many schools throughout France; indeed, in the latter part of that century Henry of Ghent remarked that the *Alexandreis* was so highly regarded that the reading of ancient poets was being reglected in favor of it. Moreover, the *Alexandreis* was influential as well as popular. Alan of Lille's oft mentioned dislike of the poem was atypical, and even his attack can stand as evidence of its appeal. The list of twelfth-century writers who knew Walter's epic and make allusions to it in their work includes, in addition to Alan, Matthew of Vendôme, Nigellus Wireker, Henry of Settimello, Joseph of Exeter, and Eberhard of Bethune. But perhaps the most impressive indication of the success of the poem lies in the number of vernacular versions of the life of Alexander that were based on it. Walter's narrative is the principal source of thirteenth-century poems in Middle Dutch (*Alexanders Geesten* by Jakob van Maerlant), Spanish (the *Libro de Alexan-*

---

(2) On Walter's reputation and its connection with his literary output while at Châtillon, see Karl Strecker, «Walter von Châtillon und seine Schule,» *Zeitschrift für deutsches Altertum* 64 (1927): 97-103, 161-168.

dre), Middle High German (Ulrich von Eschenbach's *Alexander*), and Old Czech. In the same century Brand Jonsson made a prose translation of Walter's epic into Icelandic (3).

Walter's mastery of the epic genre has won praise also from modern critics. Bolgar, for example, calls him «no pedestrian imitator» and says that he «shows a genuine appreciation of the overall form and characteristics of his genre.» To Bezzola, Walter is «un des plus brillants parmi les grands 'humanistes' du XIIe siècle, profond connaisseur des classiques qu'il imite couramment sans les copier;» and Malkiel offers what may fairly be called the widely held view that the *Alexandreis* is the best medieval imitation of a classical epic (4). These opinions are representative of those expressing admiration for Walter's achievement. Praise of the *Alexandreis* has centered almost exclusively upon Walter's *imitatio*, an important aspect of the poem to be sure, but one with which—because its excellence is generally accepted—I will deal rather briefly. After that discussion I will consider at length a neglected aspect of the

---

(3) Manitius, *op. cit.*, pp. 653, 740, 800, 813, 928; see also Christensen, *op. cit.*, pp. 166-168. On the critical reception and the influence of the *Alexandreis* George Cary, *The Medieval Alexander*, edited by D. J. A. Ross (Cambridge, 1956), is invaluable. The unkind words of Alan of Lille are from *Anticlaudianus*, 166-169:
> Maevius in coelos audens os ponere mutum,
> gesta ducis Macedum tenebrosi carminis umbra
> pingere dum temptat, in primo limine fessus
> haeret, et ignavam queritur torpescere musam...

(4) R. R. Bolgar, *The Classical Heritage and its Beneficiaries* (London, 1954), pp. 220-221; R. R. Bezzola, *Les origines et la formation de la littérature courtoise en occident 500-1200* III.1 (Paris, 1967), p. 404; Maria Rosa Lida de Malkiel, *L'Idée de la gloire dans la tradition occidentale* (Paris, 1968), p. 128. Others who have praised Walter's *imitatio* include C. Giordano, *Alexandreis, poema di Gautier da Châtillon* (Naples, 1917), p. 26; J. de Ghellinck, *L'Essor de la littérature latine au XIIe siècle* (Brussels, 1955), p. 436; Raby, *Secular Latin Poetry*, Volume II (Oxford, 1957), p. 72. Christensen's book remains the most thorough study of Walter's use of his models; however, Fritz Peter Knapp, *Similitudo* (Vienna, 1975), pp. 227-267, contains a useful analysis of Walter's imitative technique with regard to similes.

epic—Walter's originality in adapting the genre to a Christian theme.

Walter's recreation of the epic genre differs from Gerald's not in kind but in complexity, and this complexity is primarily a function of length; for the more than 5,000 lines of the *Alexandreis* allow Walter to incorporate many if not all of the features of style and content associated with Latin epic after Vergil. The rules of large scale Vergilian imitation, so to speak, had been laid down by Statius and Lucan. The *Thebaid*, in particular, can be described as an extended allusion to the *Aeneid*; but even Lucan, who flaunts his break with the Vergilian epic, manages to utilize most of the same conventions as did Statius (5). Hence, it is appropriate to say that when Walter, for example, begins his epic with an invocation and proposition (1.1...5: gesta ducis Macetum...Musa refer), he is observing tradition rather than a specific model. For the most part, Walter's imitation is of this sort. Unlike Gerald, he models no one scene directly upon a classical exemplar. He seems to have been equally familiar with Vergil, Lucan and Statius; and the overall impression left by the *Alexandreis* is of a poet who knew well the conventions of the epic genre and who wished to demonstrate that knowledge. The main components of Walter's epic style are the simile (6), the evocative allusion, and the commonplace phrase, or topos. His language is replete with reminiscences of his classical models;

---

(5) Cf. Mario di Cesare, *Vida's «Christiad» and Vergilian Epic* (New York, 1964), pp. 218-219: «C. S. Lewis has remarked that after Vergil epic poetry could not be the same again; it is quite amazing how much the same it remained. Statius set the pattern ... showing what imitation of Vergil must attempt. That is to say, a Vergilian epic must be an epic in which all the conventional devices, or as many of them as possible, are utilized for some purpose or other and are couched in Vergilian phraseology ... After Statius ... Christian epic which assayed imitation of Vergil almost always was Statian, not Vergilian—a straight narrative adapted, or contorted, to the canonical elements and in the elaborately formal style redolent of the *Aeneid*.»

(6) A complete listing of the similes which occur in the *Alexandreis* is given in Knapp, *loc. cit.*

but most often it is Lucan rather than Vergil or Statius that the echoes in the *Alexandreis* call to mind, especially in the numerous apostrophes of which both Lucan and Walter are so fond. The topoi, which I have mentioned already in my analyses of the battles described by Sedulius and Gerald, are in essence ready-made phrases of motifs which both facilitate the composition of a scene and give it an appropriate «epic» texture. These topoi were part of Vergil's Homeric imitation, and they were used by every subsequent epic poet. They are important only when employed clumsily; and while medieval Latin epic contains many examples of such clumsiness, happily they are not to be found in the *Waltharius* or the *Alexandreis*.

The content of the *Alexandreis* is in like manner traditional. Although Walter quite understandably eschews the use of the Olympian gods (in this choice following not only his Christian beliefs but also the practice of Lucan), he does manage to include supernatural machinery—as in the role of Natura and Satan in the death of Alexander (10.6-350). He has incorporated several visions into the narrative, the most important of which is the appearance of the High Priest of Jerusalem to Alexander in a dream (1.501-537). Moreover, Walter makes much use of *ekphrasis,* particularly extended descriptions of works of art. The description of the shield of Darius (2.494-529) is one example; others are the two sarcophagi designed by Apelles (4.176-274 and 7.379-430). Walter is equally adept at depicting the artwork of nature, as in his portrait of the landscape of Issus (2.306-318) or the wealth of India (9.9-34).

Even if literary tradition did not demand the inclusion of battle scenes, one could hardly avoid them in a work on the life of Alexander. But Walter's intent to compose his narrative within the bounds of the Latin epic tradition is particularly evident in such scenes. Christensen first pointed out that instead of following his historical sources Walter employs the method of epic in his tendency to focus upon series of individual combats (7). But there is more to his method. His

---

(7) Christensen, *op. cit.,* p. 83.

treatment of the battle of Arbela in books 4 and 5 illustrates both Walter's technique and his limitations as a narrator. For the episode lacks the verve of Gerald's battles, even though Walter displays an equal knowledge of how to alter perspective in order to keep the reader's attention and how to narrow the focus in order to emphasize the prowess of his central character.

The battle scene begins as it will end with emphasis on Alexander. Troubled and undecided, he calls a council of war (4.275-373), at which he scorns the suggestion of a night attack and decides on a pitched battle in full daylight. Walter then turns briefly to the Persian side and describes the initial preparations of Darius' army, with emphasis upon the glitter of the weapons (4.379-390):

> ignibus accensis acies ardere videntur:
> sideribus certant galeae, clipeisque retusis
> invenisse pares flammas stupet arduus aether,
> et metuit fieri coelum ne terra laboret.
> nec minimum gaudet nox instar habere diei:
> nam pro sole sibi Darii datur aemula Phoebi
> cassis, et in summo lampas sedet ignea cono,
> sidera quae noctis obscurans, solaque solis
> solius radiis indignans cedere: quantum
> lumine cedit ei, tantum praeiudicat illis.
> mille micant lapides in gyrum, nullus eorum
> quem iubar ardoris non disputet esse pyropum.

Walter is almost playful in his manipulation of the topos. He builds in the notion of the light reflected from the weapons rivalling first that of the stars (sideribus certant galeae) and then of the sun (gaudet nox instar habere diei). The most brilliant light, however, is that reflected from the helmet of Darius—the eventual loser of the battle; and Walter indicates his mockery of Darius by using *annominatio* (solaque solis/ solius), one of his favorite devices, to undercut the apparent splendor of the Persian king.

Walter then interrupts the narrative of events on earth to describe a «descent from heaven» when Victory sends Sleep to the troubled and restless Alexander (4.402-453). Alexander awakes filled with confidence, and there follows the motif of the «arming of the hero» for battle (4.498-521) and Alexander's exhortation to his men. Immediately after that speech, the battle begins. In this case at least Walter, unlike Gerald (and like Lucan), pays little attention to the physical setting of the battle; but he is careful to work in the topoi of the noise of the fighting reaching the sky (4.589: it tantus ad aethera clamor) and of the «shower» of weapons (5.23: missiliumque frequens regem circumvolat imber). The latter image is used to direct our attention back to Alexander; and the rest of the scene is, with a few interruptions, his *aristeia*.

The *aristeia* of Alexander begins with two of his less demanding victims, and a picture of the carnage all around (5.29-35):

> quo feriente cadunt Eliphas Pharaone creatus,
> et Pharos Orchanides: Eliphas iaculo, Pharos ense,
> hic eques, ille pedes, Aegyptius hic, Syrus ille.
> sicca prius sterilisque diu iam flumine fusi
> sanguinis humet humus, iamque imbuit unda cruoris
> arterias Cybeles: cadit infinita vicissim
> Persarum Macetumque manus.

Walter's playfulness in dealing with commonplaces, which I mentioned above, surfaces again when he takes the opportunity to pun while describing the «earth moist with blood» (flumine fusi /sanguinis humet humus). Moreover, his mannered lingering over Eliphas and Pharos, who are after all not very important, gives the impression that the poet is perhaps more interested in his art than in a lively narrative; for these lesser warriors are but a prelude to Alexander's struggle with the giant Geon (5.38-75). Similes at the beginning and the end of this episode stress the enormous size of Alexander's foe. In the first (5.47-54) he is a wild boar standing head and shoulder above the dogs which have cornered it; in the second (5.68-71) he falls like an uproted tree. In the center is the account of his death (5.56-65):

>   ...dumque arduus ille cruentam
> erigeret clavam, clamoso gutture regi
> intonat «heus» inquit «quis te furor egit in hostem,
> Magne, giganteum? quem sidereas Iovis arces
> affectasse legis? a quo vix fulmine tandem
> tutus in aethera mansit Saturnius arce?»
> nondum finierat, agili cum torta lacerto
> pinus Alexandri medio stetit ore loquentis,
> faucibus affigens linguam, ne deroget ultra
> coelicolis.

As Geon derides Alexander's stupidity in standing up to a giant, and as he blasphemes the gods, the Macedonian hurls a spear which strikes the boaster in the mouth (pinus Alexandri medio stetit ore loquentis). This motif of a spear interrupting the exclamations of a boasting enemy may have been suggested to Walter by Statius (*Thebaid* 2.624-628). At any rate, the death blow is peculiarly appropriate; and after Geon crashes to the ground, Alexander's soldiers finish him off.

Walter now shifts our attention to the exploits of two other Greek warriors, Clitus (5.76-122) and Nicanor (5.123-182). After brief success, Clitus is killed. Nicanor, however, wreaks greater havoc among the Persians. The description of his rampage contains a pointed allusion to Lucan's *Bellum Civile*. In that epic, the shade of Julia appears in a dream to Pompey and to emphasize the coming horrors of the civil war uses the image of the Fates being hard pressed to cut the threads fast enough (3.18-19):

> vix operi cunctae dextra properante sorores
> sufficiunt, lassant rumpentes stamina Parcas.

Walter adopts this image in describing the slaughter taking place all around Nicanor (5.142-144):

> rumpere fila manu non sufficit una sororum,
> abiectaque colo Clotho Lachesisque virorum
> fata metunt, unamque duae iuvere sorores.

Again Walter seems momentarily more interested in the challenge of word-play than sword-play. So many men are dying that one sister alone is not up to the task, and the other two must leave their appointed tasks to help. Walter has taken an outlandish image and managed to outdo his model. Fierce though Nicanor is, however, he too must fall. His death and that of Clitus surely are meant in part as counterpoints to the continuing success of Alexander, whose deeds fill the rest of the episode (5.183-282). Like Gerald, then, Walter has composed his battle scene with a steadily narrowing focus meant at last to emphasize the martial prowess of his central character . Nevertheless, this episode from the *Alexandreis* lacks the vigor of the earlier epic. The real skill in Walter's depiction of what happens at Issus lies in his foreshadowing of ultimate failure within Alexander's apparent success. But I must defer that discussion for the moment.

As I did with the *Waltharius,* I will now examine Walter's artistry in the composition of one simile. In Book 1, he compares Alexander to a young lion raging at the sight of a herd of deer (1.49-58):

> qualiter Hyrcanis cum forte leunculus arvis
> cornibus elatis videt ire ad pabula cervos,
> cui nondum totos descendit robur in armos,
> nec pede firmus adhuc, nec dentibus asper aduncis:
> palpitat, et vacuum ferit improba lingua palatum,
> effunditque prius animo quam dente cruorem,
> pigritiamque pedum redimit matura voluntas:
> sic puer effrenus totus bacchatur in arma,
> invalidusque manu gerit alto corde leonem,
> et praeceps teneros audacia praevenit annos.

Impatiently the cub strikes his tongue against his empty palate (vacuum ferit improba lingua palatum) and imagines himself killing the deer (effunditque prius animo quam dente cruorem). There exist several possible «sources» for this simile. In Book 1 of the *Bellum Civile,* Lucan compares Caesar to a lion (1.205-212):

> ...sicut squalentibus arvis
> aestiferae Libyes viso leo comminus hoste
> susedit dubius, totam cum colligit iram;
> mox, ubi se saevae stimulavit verbere caudae
> erexitque iubam et vasto grave murmur hiatu
> infremuit, tum, torta levis si lancea Mauri
> haereat aut latum subeant venabula pectus,
> per ferrum tanti securus volneris exit.

Although the circumstances are similar, in that both lions rage at the sight of prey, this image contains no mention of the lion's desire to spill blood which is prominent in the passage from the *Alexandreis*. References to blood and thirst do appear in the next simile of Lucan's epic (1.327-332):

> utque ferae tigres nunquam posuere furorem,
> quas nemore Hyrcano matrum dum lustra secuntur,
> altus caesorum pavit cruor armentorum,
> sic et Sullanum solito tibi lambere ferrum
> durat, Magne, sitis. nullus semel ore receptus
> pollutas patitur sanguis mansuescere fauces.

Lucan's reference here is to Pompey; but he is an old man, and he has actually drunk the blood which the young lion Alexander still only imagines. Indeed, the notion of a young animal spilling blood in its imagination may owe something to the *Punica* of Silius Italicus (4.333-336):

> ...illa [tigris] pererrat
> desertas victrix valles, iamque ora reducto
> paulatim nudat rictu, ut praesentia mandens
> corpora, et immani stragem meditatur hiatu.

It seems more likely, however, that Walter was influenced by a simile from Claudian's *de III cons. Hon.* (77-80):

> ut leo, quem fulvae matris spelunca tegebat,
> uberibus solitum pasci, cum crescere sensit
> unque pedes et terga iubis et dentibus ora;
> iam negat imbelles epulas...

Here, as in Walter's simile, we have a young lion; moreover, both lions, though unable actually to kill their prey, are eager to end their dependence on the food of cubs. The sheer wealth of animal similes in the Latin epic tradition makes it possible, of course, to point to more similes bearing a resemblance to the one in question. The significant point, however, is that Walter borrowed none. The *leunculus* image is very much his own creation. It is effective in its immediate context; in addition, as we shall see, it stands at the beginning of a series of four extended animal similes applied to Alexander which form a coherent pattern that helps emphasize the thematic structure of the whole work.

Finally, I must restate the importance of the influence of Lucan upon Walter as an epic poet. Although he modestly cites Vergil as his model (prol. 19-20: non enim me arbitror Mantuano vate meliorem), his style and his conception of epic owe more to Lucan. In the words which Eberhard of Bethune used about Walter's narrative, *lucet Alexander Lucani luce*. Walter's language abounds in reminiscences of the *Bellum Civile*; his frequent use of moralizing apostrophes reflects his admiration for Lucan; indeed, it seems hardly by chance that Walter divided the *Alexandreis* into ten, not twelve books (8). Yet Walter's choice of Lucan as a model should strike the reader familiar with the *Bellum Civile* as odd. Lucan, after all, could hardly be described as an admirer of Alexander. Of all the attacks in classical literature against Alexander none is more withering than the denunciation which appears at the beginning of the final book of the *Bellum Civile* (10.20-52). Alexander was, for Lucan, a madman and a bandit whom he cannot even bring himself to call by name (20.20-28):

> illic Pellaei proles vesana Philippi,
> felix praedo, iacet terrarum vindice fato
> raptus: sacratis totum spargenda per orbem

---

(8) Knapp deserves credit for emphasizing the importance of Lucan as a model for Walter, though he fails to pursue the implications of this fact.

> membra viri posuere adytis; Fortuna pepercit
> manibus, et regni duravit ad ultima fatum.
> nam sibi libertas umquam si redderet orbem,
> ludibrio servatus erat, non utile mundo
> editus exemplum, terras tot posse sub uno
> esse viro.

Alexander's famous luck spared his body, which should have been ripped apart and scattered over the world as a reminder of tyranny. He left a bad example to the world (non utile mundo/editus exemplum), that so many lands can be subject to one man. After summarizing Alexander's career, Lucan points out that only death halted his advance (10.37-45):

> ...non illi flammae nec undae
> nec sterilis Lybye nec Syrticus obstitit Hammon.
> isset in occasus mundi devexa secutus
> ambissetque polos Nilumque a fonte bibisset:
> occurrit suprema dies, Naturaque solum
> hunc potuit finem vaesano ponere regi;
> qui secum invidia, quo totum ceperat orbem,
> abstulit imperium, nulloque herede relicto
> totius fati lacerandas praebuit urbes.

In discussing Alexander's death, Lucan makes the comment —one of considerable importance, as we shall see, for the reader of Walter's epic—that only Natura was able to put an end to the mad king (Naturaque solum / hunc potuit finem vaesano ponere regi).

If we wish to accept the widely held view that Walter composed his epic to hold up Alexander as a model of heroic excellence, we must face this paradox: why choose as his model an epic poet who vehemently hated Alexander? Walter himself forces us to confront the issue at the conclusion of the *Alexandreis* when he repeats the notion of Alexander as an *exemplum* (10.448-454):

> Magnus in exemplo est: cui non suffecerat orbis,
> sufficit exciso defossa marmore terra

> quinque pedum fabricata domus, qua nobile corpus
> exigua requievit humo, donec Ptolemaeus,
> cui legis Aegyptum in partem cessisse, verendi
> depositum fati toti venerabile mundo
> transtulit ad dictam de nomine principis urbem.

The evocation of Lucan through the reference to Alexander as an *exemplum* (Magnus in exemplo est) is strengthened by Walter's use of another theme which figures prominently in the *Bellum Civile*. Walter remarks that now the confined space of a tomb is enough for Alexander, for whom once the world had not sufficed (cui non suffecerat orbis) (9). This same phrase appears at two important points in Lucan's epic. Caesar, when confronted by an uprising among his soldiers, uses the words (5.356: quibus hic non sufficit orbis)—albeit with fierce irony—to describe his weary and resentful men. Later the phrase is applied to Caesar himself (10.454-460):

> quem non violasset Alanus,
> non Scytha, non fixo qui ludit in hospite Maurus,
> hic cui Romani spatium non sufficit orbis,
> parvaque regna putet Tyriis cum Gadibus Indos,
> ceu puer inbellis, ceu captis femina muris,
> quarit tuta domus; spem vitae in limine clauso
> ponit, et incerto lustrat vagus atria cursu.

Both Walter and Lucan use their final reference to the notion of sufficiency with ironic intent. Walter contrasts the whole world with the narrow confines of a tomb (quinque pedum... domus); Caesar's boundless ambition is contrasted with the small room of a house (domus) which Lucan calls an «unworthy hiding place» (10.441: degeneres passus latebras). Is this connection of Alexander with the Caesar of the *Bellum Civile* without significance? If so, why does Walter establish it so carefully? Is it part of a larger design which has gone

---

(9) This theme has its roots in the *Suasoriae*; see M. P. O. Morford, *The Poet Lucan* (Oxford, 1967), pp. 16-17.

unnoticed by critics, or an example of a lack of focus on Walter's part? And given Walter's admiration for Lucan, should we as readers not take into account the fact that the *Bellum Civile* was seen by many medieval commentators as containing praise uttered *per ironiam*?

Unfortunately, such questions have largely been ignored, especially by those who dismiss the *Alexandreis* as unsuccessful or «merely imitative.» The sharpest attacks on the poem have centered on the so-called episodic nature of the narrative, and on Walter's inability to weave what is seen as a series of disconnected episodes into a coherent whole. Haskins, for example, lumps Walter's effort with Joseph of Exeter's *Ylias* and the «interminable» *Troie* of their contemporary Benoît as typical of the degeneration of the classical epic tradition (10). Only Christensen has seen any controlling design in the narrative; he notes that Walter omits all Alexander's minor campaigns and battles in order to concentrate the reader's attention on the two great struggles—between Alexander and Darius, Alexander and Porus (11). The more common view is that expressed recently by Knapp, whose appreciation for elements of the epic is outweighed by his dislike of its episodic structure, or lack thereof. Knapp's harsh final judgment it that «ein flüchtiger Vergleich mit Vergil und selbst Lucan zeigt schon das Unvermögen des Dichters, die versifizierte Historiographie zum Epos zu wandeln» (12). The *Alexandreis,* in sum, appears to several critics to be little more than a chronicle epic, that is, a straightforward recounting of events which the author gives heroic proportions by including the conventional machinery of epic narrative. In this view the *Alexandreis* is raised from mediocrity, if it is, only by Walter's admiration for the exploits and *magnanimitas* of Alexander.

---

(10) Charles Homer Haskins, *The Renaissance of the Twelfth Century* (Cambridge, Mass., 1927; repr. Cleveland, 1964), p. 266.
(11) Christensen, *op. cit.*, pp. 107-109.
(12) Knapp, *op. cit.*, p. 266. See my review of this book in *Speculum*, Volume 52, Number 4 (1977): 1010-1013.

Knapp's conclusion, though wrong I think, contains an important reminder that the *Alexandreis* is essentially a historical epic. Walter is dealing with the Alexander of history, not of marvelous legend. His primary source of information about Alexander is the *Historiae Alexandri Magni Macedonis* composed by Quintus Curtius probably in the second half of the first century AD. Where information from Curtius was lacking, he made use of Justin's epitome of the *Historiae Philippicae* by the Augustan historian Pompeius Trogus. His sources include as well Julius Valerius, Josephus, Isidore of Seville, and one might add Lucan. Curtius, however, is the most important. He portrays Alexander as a man of noble character who was corrupted by success. He argues that the vices of the Persians conquered Alexander even though their weapons could not (6.2.1: quem arma Persarum non fregerant, vitia vicerunt). Central to Curtius' treatment of the downfall of Alexander is the role of Fortuna. He portrays Alexander's luck as unfailingly good (cf. 8.3.1: Fortuna, indulgendo ei numquam fatigata). In speaking of Fortuna, Curtius marvels at the constancy of her protection of Alexander (10.5.32: quotiens temere in pericula vectum perpetua felicitate protexit!). Yet Curtius perceives in Alexander's luck the seeds of his destruction. His Fortuna is seen as the cause of many of the vices of which he can be accused (10.5.26: bona naturae eius fuisse, vitia vel Fortunae vel aetatis).

The role of luck (Fortuna, *tychē*) was an important feature of ancient portraits of Alexander, and was stressed particularly by his Stoic and Peripatetic critics. I have alluded to two aspects of this theme in Curtius' account: that Alexander owed his success to an uncharacteristic constancy of Fortuna's favor, but also that such constant good luck was responsible for the deterioration of his character. Among Roman historians who discuss Alexander, Livy (9.17-19) also argued that Alexander was victimized by his prosperity, which caused him to give way to drunkenness and anger. Livy repeats as well the Peripatetic view that Alexander was lucky to die before his Fortuna could change for the worse. This theme was picked up by Christian writers, particularly those trying to point a moral from the story of Alexander's career. A typical example of this kind of moralizing interpretation is to be found in the Monk's Tale from Chaucer's *Canterbury Tales*. Fortune is mentioned four times in the forty lines devoted specifically to Alexander. Alexander's uncommonly good luck is cited (2643: Fortune hym made the heir of hire honour); but his death is described in terms of her fickleness (3848-3852):

> O worthy, gentil Alisandre, allas,
> that evere sholde fallen swich a cas!
> empoysened of thyn owene folk thou weere;
> thy sys Fortune hath turned into aas,
> and yet for thee ne weep she never a teere.

The image of Fortune playing a dice game is a common one, and one used to good effect by Walter, I should add. Later, after the monk tells the story of Julius Caesar, he thus concludes (2719-2726):

> Lucan, to thee this storie I recomende,
> and to Swetoun, and to Valerie also,
> that of this storie writen word and ende,
> how that to thise grete conqueroures two
> Fortune was first freend, and sitthe foo.
> no man ne truste upon hire favour longe,
> but have hire in awayt for everemoo;
> witnesse on alle thise conqueroures stronge.

The fact that Alexander died, as every man must, makes him susceptible to being an *exemplum* of the fickleness of Fortune. Indeed, among later medieval writers it appears that the theme of Alexander as a plaything of Fortune is associated primarily with stories of his death. This rather limited connection may explain the relatively few illustrations in medieval art of Alexander himself on the famous Wheel of Fortune (13).

---

(13) Cary, *op. cit.*, is a rich source of information for medieval

Fortuna plays a prominent role not only in Walter's primary historical source, Curtius, but also in his main literary model. Fortuna is the principal divine force in the *Bellum Civile* (14). It encompasses the role that a number of gods and goddesses fulfill in the *Aeneid* and *Thebaid*. Caesar is victorious, in Lucan's view, because he is Fortuna's favorite; and he in turn willingly follows Fortuna (1.226: te, Fortuna, sequor). Caesar's adversary Pompey also sees Fortuna as the controlling force operating in human affairs. Although Pompey perceives, as Caesar does not, the capricious and unjust nature of Fortuna, he too allows himself to be ruled by her. A third individual linked by Lucan to Fortuna is, of course, Alexander, to whose Fortuna Lucan makes specific reference (10.23-24: Fortuna pepercit/manibus). We are reminded, however, that Lucan hated both Alexander and Caesar, the two *filii Fortunae*; and we must continue to ponder the significance of this reliance upon Lucan by the author of an epic about Alexander.

In conclusion, although elements of the *Alexandreis* have been much praised, on the whole Walter's epic has been dismissed by modern critics as either a failure or at best a pleasant entertainment. It is assumed that Walter's purpose in composing the *Alexandreis* was to glorify Alexander the Great. This view is stated with vigor by Cary, whose assertion that «the spell of Alexander's conquests» had fallen upon Walter and that Walter made his Alexander into a godlike hero» has found widespread acceptance. Associated with this inter-

---

attitudes concerning Alexander. On Fortuna, still useful is Howard R. Patch, *The Goddess Fortuna in Medieval Literature* (Cambridge, Mass., 1927). Every student of medieval literature is indebted to F. P. Pickering's work on the place of Fortuna in Christian historical thought. Pickering's thesis is stated most fully in *Augustinus oder Boethius?* I. Einführender Teil (Philologische Studien und Quellen 39: Berlin, 1967). For a compilation, episode by episode, of Walter's use of his historical sources, see Christensen, *op. cit.*, pp. 212-216.

(14) See W.-H. Friedrich, «Cato, Caesar und Fortuna bei Lucan,» *Hermes* 73 (1938): 391-423; an excellent discussion of the role of Fortuna in the *Bellum Civile* appears in Frederick M. Ahl, *Lucan: An Introduction* (Ithaca, New York, 1976), pp. 286-305.

pretation is the assumption that the *Alexandreis* is, in the main, escapist literature; that is, that Walter, like an earlier day William Morris, is, in Raby's words, «taking refuge from the present in a more spacious world, a world of heroes and kings, of antique virtue and of superhuman endeavour.» To summarize, the *Alexandreis* is regarded by many as a skillful recreation of the epic form, but a barren one, which Walter, perhaps prompted by a nostalgic vision of a *temps perdu,* composed to laud Alexander as the noblest available model of heroic excellence (15).

I intend to show, however, that up to now praise and criticism alike have been based on a mistaken notion of Walter's stance with regard to the epic tradition, for his *imitatio* is not so straightforward, nor is the meaning of his epic so obvious. A detailed examination of the narrative, with particular attention to the interrelated themes of *gloria* and *fortuna,* will make clear both the ironic tone which pervades it and the criticism of Alexander which gives it thematic unity. We will see that the *Alexandreis,* like the *Waltharius,* is fundamentally a mocking epic. As Gerald seemed at first to be offering a new model of Christian heroism, so the Alexander of Walter's narrative seems at first to be «of knyghthod and of fredom flour.» However, Walter too undercuts and mocks the apparent excellence of his protagonist. We will see that when he states at the conclusion of his work *Magnus in exemplo est* (10.448), it is cautionary *exemplum*; for Walter stresses the limitations

---

(15) Cary, *op. cit.,* p. 173; Raby, *op. cit.,* II, p. 79. Cf. Bolgar, «Hero or Anti-Hero?» in *Concepts of the Hero in the Middle Ages and the Renaissance,* ed. Norman T. Burns and Christopher J. Regan (Albany, New York, 1975), p. 125: «a fashion ... to glorify merely human courage and success (a fashion that gave us Walter of Châtillon's *Alexandreis* and the several versions of the tale of Troy).» Christensen also stresses Walter's admiration for Alexander, *op. cit.,* p. 109. Only Knapp, *op. cit.,* p. 250, has seen even «ambivalence» in Walter's attitude toward Alexander. A recent dismissal of the *Alexandreis* as a simple story without deeper purpose is made by James J. Sheridan, *Alan of Lille*: *Anticlaudianus* (Toronto, 1973), p. 36.

of Alexander's greatness. More accurately, Walter uses Alexander to criticize the outmoded heroic cast of mind which focuses on the transient glory of this mutable world to the exclusion of higher values. This criticism provides an underlying structure that ties together the series of episodes of which the narrative is composed.

The *Alexandreis* begins with emphasis on glory. In his proposition, Walter stresses not only the glory which Alexander won but also how much more he would have won had he lived longer (1.1-8):

> gesta ducis Macetum totum digesta per orbem,
> quam large dispersit opes, quo milite Porum
> vicerit et Darium, quo principe Graecia victrix
> risit et a Persis rediere tributa Corinthum,
> Musa refer: qui si senio non fractus inermi
> pollice fatorum iustos vixisset in annos,
> Caesareos numquam loqueretur fama triumphos,
> totaque Romuleae squaleret gloria gentis.

This statement of the superiority of his subject matter to that of the Roman poets (totaque Romuleae squaleret gloria gentis) contrasts with the modesty which Walter affects in his prologue. The theme of glory is continued in our introduction to Alexander as an impatient youth chafing for war (1.27-32):

> nondum prodierat naturae plana tenellis
> infruticans lanugo pilis, Martique parabat
> dissimiles proferre genas, cum pectore toto
> arma puer sitiens Darium dare iura Pelasgis
> gentibus imperiique iugo patris arva prementem
> audit, et indignans his vocibus exprimit iram.

Not yet a man, Alexander is eager to avenge the wrongs inflicted on the Greeks by Darius. Yet this first statement concerning him has a potential for irony which will be realized at the conclusion of the poem; the reader acquainted with the fact that Alexander died «empoysened of thyn owene folk» will see that potential in Walter's description of the young boy thirsting (sitiens) for arms. This impatience is the cause of the anger (his vocibus exprimit iram) which dominates Alexander's first speech (1.33-47). He recalls that his ancestor Hercules when still an infant killed the two snakes which attacked him in his crib (16). And his final complaint (1.46-47: semperne putabor / Nectanabi proles?) speaks to Alexander's hatred of anonymity. Walter then draws this part of the episode to a close with the fine simile (1.49-58)—which I discussed earlier and to which I will return—comparing Alexander to a young lion performing in his imagination deeds which he is not yet able to accomplish in fact.

After youth, age: Aristotle enters and, perceiving Alexander's anger (1.73: accusabat enim occultam igneus iram), offers him encouragement and advice. This speech (1.82-183), like the rest of the scene, is apparently Walter's own invention. Although mistakenly dismissed by Raby as merely «an interpolated school-exercise» (17), it is actually the key passage in the design of the whole epic. It serves two functions. Not only is it an explication of the nature of heroic virtue, but it also sets the groundwork for Walter's attack on the inadequacy of that definition. The speech is carefully structured. It begins and ends with mentions of Alexander's anger. Moreover, with his first sentence Aristotle declares his role to be that of a teacher (1.82-84):

> indue mente virum, Macedo puer, arma capesse,
> materiam virtutis habes, rem profer in actum,
> quoque modo id possis, aures adverte, docebo.

Alexander has a potential for heroic excellence (materiam virtutis) which Aristotle will teach him how to realize (rem profer

---

(16) See A. R. Anderson, «Herakles and his Successors,» *Harvard Studies in Classical Philology* 39 (1928): 7-58.
(17) Raby, *op. cit.* II, p. 73; for a source of the ideas expressed by Aristotle see R. Wisbey, «Die Aristotlesrede bei Walter von Châtillon und Rudolf von Ems,» *ZfdA* 85 (1954-1955): 304-311.

in actum...docebo). After he completes his instruction, Walter calls Aristotle a *monitor virtutis* (1.184). In between, Alexander's tutor discusses the nature of *virtus*, the vices which hinder one from attaining it, and the reward in store for the individual who does attain it.

As implied above (materiam virtutis habes), Aristotle's discourse turns on the philosophical idea that inner strength, not possessions confers nobility on a man (1.99-104):

> quem vero morum, non rerum copia ditat,
> quem virtus extollit, habet quod praeferat auro,
> quo patriae vitium redimat, quod conferat illi
> et genus et formam: virtus non quaeritur extra:
> non eget externis, qui moribus intus abundat:
> nobilitas sola est, animum quae moribus ornat.

After stating the basic notion that virtue is an inner quality (virtus non quaeritur extra), Aristotle turns to a discussion of those vices which can undermine the *stabilem mentem* (1.107) of the heroic man. When he points to *avaritia* (1.111-114) as the first of these, one expects a discussion of that sin. Instead, Aristotle offers Alexander advice on the proper conduct of a general in battle. This section on martial valor begins (1.115: parce humili, gracilis oranti frange superbum) with an evocation of Anchises' famous injunction to Aeneas (*Aeneid* 6.853: parcere subjectis et debellare superbos). It concludes with a return to the theme of avarice; for Aristotle urges Alexander to be generous to his soldiers (1.146-151):

> thesauros aperi, plue donativa maniplis,
> vulneribus crudis et corde tumentibus aegro
> muneris infundas oleum, gazisque reclusis
> unge animos donis, aurique appone liquorem.
> haec aegrae menti poterit medicina mederi:
> sic inopi largusque medetur avaro.

This advice, surely a reference to the *largitas* for which Alexander was famous in the twelfth century, is also a warning against greed; for Aristotle suggests that generosity succeeds through its appeal to the greed of lesser men (1.156; munus enim mores confert, irretit avaros). Indeed, he then makes that warning explicit by saying that neither a wall nor weapons can protect an avaricious leader (1.163: non murus non arma ducem tutantur avarum).

The other vices against which Aristotle warns his pupil (1.164: cetera quid moneam?) are *luxuries* and *amor*. His complaint about each is that it destroys rational control (1.167-168: si Baccho Venerique vacas, qui cetera subdis / sub iuga venisti). Aristotle's original emphasis on *virtus* as an interior quality is recalled in his language concerning drunkenness and sexual passion, both of which weaken a man's inner strength (1.172: rigidos enervant haec duo mores). Of the former he says *te emolliat intus* (1.164); of the latter, *mens hebet interius* (1.170). Alexander's *monitor virtutis* ends his speech with an admonition against the emotion the sight of which prompted him to address the boy (1.181-183):

> vindictam differ, donec pertranseat ira,
> nec meminisse velis odii post verbera: si sic
> vixeris, aeternum extendes per saecula nomen.

These concluding words also express the reward for the man who realizes his potential for greatness. The reward is glory —his name prolonged forever (aeternum extendes per saecula nomen). No other enticement is mentioned; for Alexander, none is needed.

Aristotle's speech is crucial to a proper understanding of the *Alexandreis*. It describes the *virtus* which Alexander will strive to achieve; but despite achieving it he will fail to become a model of heroic excellence for the Christian world. For Walter has embedded in this discourse the means by which he will expose the inadequacy, by Christian standards, of that *virtus*. I refer to the numerous allusions within the speech to Boethius' *De Consolatione Philosophiae*, a work with which Walter could reasonably have assumed that every reader of his epic would be familiar. Boethius was, after all, an *auctor,* a writer considered to be authoritative for the genre in which he composed and a model worthy of imitation. The *Consolation* was much used in the schools, a fact which is hardly suprising (18). For the educative appeal of a dialogue in which Lady Philosophy encourages and instructs a despairing man is self-evident. I have mentioned the close association between Alexander and Fortuna; and of course among the principal themes of the *Consolation* is the complaint of Philosophy that men mistakenly regard tangible things (among them power and fame), which are by their nature ephemeral, as true goods. Sunk in temporal cares and the quest for external possessions, they neglect the light of contemplation, and follow instead sensual pleasures. Such men place themselves in the power of Fortuna, to whom are attributed alternations between worldly prosperity and adversity. Those on Fortuna's ever turning wheel are never secure; for if they are raised to prosperity, they know that soon they are to be lowered again. Although Boethius argues later that Fortuna, strictly speaking, is an illusion (since nothing really happens by chance in a divinely ordained universe), nonetheless Boethius offers a vivid—and not forgotten—picture of her control over those who place their lives on her wheel by involving themselves exclusively in the transitory world of created things.

The first identifiable Boethian reference in Aristotle's speech occurs in his argument that *virtus* is an inner quality rather than a reflection of external possessions (1.102...103: virtus non quaeritur extra...qui moribus intus abundat). Two passages from the *Consolation* are pertinent here (2. pr. 4...pr. 5):

> quid igitur o mortales extra petitis intra vos positam felicitatem...itane autem nullum est proprium vobis atque insitum bonum ut in externis ac sepositis rebus bona vestra quaeratis?

---

(18) John Block Friedman, *Orpheus in the Middle Ages*

Both passages contain the contrast between external and internal goods, and both decry the foolishness of seeking outside what is obtainable only within. In like manner, Aristotle's warning against avarice begins with a reference to the *Consolation*. His explanation that greed has the power to undermine a stable mind (stabilem mentem) recalls the Boethian explanation of the only stability that does exist (4. pr. 6):

> omnium generatio rerum cunctusque mutabilium naturarum progressus et quidquid aliquo movetur modo, causas, ordinem, formas ex divinae mentis stabilitate sortitur.

Notice that Philosophy, speaking here, is drawing the distinction between the mutable nature of the things of this world (mutabilium naturarum progressus) and the stability of the divine order (divinae mentis stabilitate). The power which rules those obsessed with the transient goods of the mutable world is, according to the *Consolation*, Fortuna. And the next Boethian allusion in Aristotle's speech is to her. I refer to his description of war, the field of action in which Alexander is to win his glory, as a game (1.118: dum luditur alea Martis). Games of chance are of course natural and much used images of Fortuna in medieval literature. We have already encountered one example in Chaucer's reference to dice (thy sys Fortune hath turned to aas), and we will see that Walter makes dicing a recurrent image of his epic. But more important for the moment is the association of simply playing (luditur) with the portrait of Fortuna in the *Consolation*. Consider her own words (2. pr. 2):

> haec nostra vis est, hunc continuum ludum ludimus; rotam volubili orbe versamus, infima summis summa

---

(Cambridge, Mass., 1970), p. 96. The definitive study of the influence of Boethius on medieval literature is Pierre Courcelle, *La Consolation de Philosophie dans la Tradition Littéraire, Antécédents et Posterité de Boèce* (Paris, 1967).

infimis mutare gaudemus. ascende si placet, sed ea lege ne utique cum ludicri mei ratio poscet, descendere iniuriam putes.

Fortuna is playing a continuous game (hunc continuum ludum ludimus). That game is the turning of her wheel; and the rule of the game (ludicri mei ratio) is instability. We will see many references in the *Alexandreis* to this important self-description. With this one reference, however, Walter establishes the game of war as a part of Fortuna's larger game, a connection of considerable significance for our understanding of Alexander's outlook on life.

An image which is prominent in the *Consolation* likewise appears in Aristotle's advice to Alexander concerning the *largitas* necessary for a successful leader. Throughout the *Consolation* Philosophy is presented as the doctor whose medicine will cure Boethius' sickness, that is, his obsession with temporal goods (1. pr. 2: «sed medicinae,» inquit «tempus est quam querulae»). Yet Aristotle argues that earthly riches themselves can be a medicine for a sick mind (1.150: haec aegrae menti... medicina). This whole section seems to be a conscious perversion (cf. 1.151: sic inopi dives largusque medetur avaro) of Boethius' exhortation to generosity (2 pr. 5: avaritia semper odiosos, claros largitas facit).

Finally, let us consider the very reward of *virtus* which Aristotle holds out to the young Alexander—worldly glory, a name extended *per saecula*. We have seen in Juvencus' preface one Christian refutation of the notion that secular literature can provide «eternal» fame. That same misconception is attacked strongly in the *Consolation*. Boethius tells Philosophy that he has always desired a life of action because he feared a «silent» *virtus* in his old age (2 pr. 7: sed materiam gerendis rebus optavimus quo ne virtus tacita consenesceret). Philosophy replies that the desire for glory is a vain and empty thing (2. pr. 7: exilis et totius vacua ponderis); but even more interesting is her contention that glory holds attraction for minds «not yet fully brought to excellence by the perfecting of virtues» (2. pr.

7: mentes sed nondum ad extremam manum virtutum perductas). Later in the same conversation we encounter a withering attack on the desire for fame, promised by Aristotle, which Alexander proclaims to be his greatest desire later in the epic. In the words of Lady Philosophy (2. pr. 7):

> sed quam multos clarissimos suis temporibus viros scriptorum inops delevit oblivio! quamquam quid ipsa scripta proficiant, quae cum suis auctoribus premit longior atque obscura vetustas? vos vero immortalitatem vobis propagare videmini, cum futuri famam temporis cogitatis. quod si aeternitatis infinita spatia pertractes, quid habes quod de nominis tui diuturnitate laeteris?

Our deeds, recorded or not, are doomed ultimately to oblivion. Philosophy argues that it is foolish to imagine that writers can grant immortality to one's actions, since literature itself is ephemeral. She goes on to say that in comparison with the infinite reaches of eternity, the mere prolonging of one's name (nominis tui diuturnitate) is little cause for rejoicing. After an illustration of the vastness of true eternity, she states (2. pr. 7):

> ita fit ut quamlibet prolixi temporis fama, si cum inexhausta aeternitate cogitetur, non parva sed plane nulla esse videatur.

Fame, secular fame, of however long a duration, when considered against eternity, is exposed as «not a small thing but almost nothing at all» (non parva sed plane nulla). She concludes with a statement concerning the correct attitude of a man, on the point of dying, toward glory. But my discussion of that important remark must wait until the moment in the *Alexandreis* when Alexander himself, on the brink of death, makes reference to it.

In sum, the clustering of allusions to the *Consolation* in the *Alexandreis* serves a purpose much like that served by Gerald's clustering of allusions to the *Psychomachia* in his epic. In Aristotle's long discourse, Walter has at once given a «classical» definition of *virtus,* and established the means of his attack on it. In a sense, one can say that the continuing theme of the *Alexandreis* is a refutation of the reference to Aristotle at the conclusion of his speech as being a *monitor virtutis* (1.184). On the contrary, the reader of the epic will be led to a recognition that Boethius' exclamation in the *Consolation* (1. pr. 3: omnium magistra virtutum) is to a far better teacher of a far superior doctrine.

The scene between Aristotle and Alexander continues with Alexander's response to the words of his tutor. That response Walter describes in terms of *gloria*. The youth drinks in the lesson, and his mind is goaded by a desire for praise (1.189: laudum stimulis). As Alexander earlier had reproached himself in comparison to Hercules, now Walter likens him to Neoptolemus wishing to do what even his father Achilles hardly could accomplish (1.198-199: tunc tanta videres / velle Neoptolemum quae vix expleret Achilles). However, Aristotle's emphasis upon rational control seems to have had less impact, for Alexander prepares to rage (1.201: insanire) against first the Persians, then the world. And thus ends the carefully designed prefatory episode (1.1-202) of the *Alexandreis*. Walter has introduced Alexander. He has also presented the basic elements of his criticism of Alexander's values—and by extension the values of the classical heroic tradition. It is this criticism, not the gests themselves of Alexander, that is the subject of the rest of the narrative.

In the other major episode of Book One—Alexander's visit to the tomb of Achilles (1.452-538)—Walter establishes that a desire for glory and a recognition of the power of Fortuna are the essential features of Alexander's heroic outlook. The intervening lines, however, contain two scenes which are worthy of note. The first of these two scenes describes the attempt by Cleadas to dissuade Alexander from destroying Thebes. He reminds the young king of Aristotle's advice (1.328-335):

> clara deum proles Macedo, fortissime regum,
> cui favet astrorum series, cui quatuor orbis
> climata despondent filo properante sorores,
> cuius, ut invictus victis et parcere scires
> supplicibus victor et debellare rebelles,
> divinis toties monitis armavit anhelum
> pectus Aristoteles, tune hanc, rex, funditus urbem
> exitio delere paras?

His words evoke those of Aristotle's discourse. The phrase *victis et parcere scires...et debellare rebelles* recalls the admonition *parce humili...frange superbum* (1.115). Later in his speech Cleadas urges Alexander, to whom Aristotle had stressed the importance of *pietas* (1.178: nec desit pietas), that he «learn to be kind to the conquered» (1.341: disce pius victis). Cleadas' unsuccessful plea concludes with the assertion that the kingdom not propped by clemency is unstable (1.342: instabile est regnum, quod non clementia firmit). To a degree, of course, this *sententia* is true; but we should at the same time remember that, in Boethian terms, no kingdom of the sort Alexander intends, even if strengthened by *clementia,* can ever be truly stable.

The second passage of interest occurs as part of the description of the arrival of Alexander and his army in Asia (1.440-441):

> «iam satis est,» inquit, «socii, mihi sufficit una
> haec regio: Europam vobis patriamque relinquo.»

Alexander utters these words as soon as he catches sight of land. The scene is inspired by the following portion of Justin's narrative (11.5.4-5):

> adunato deinde evercitu naves onerat, unde conspecta Asia incredibili ardore mentis accensus duodecim deorum aras in belli vota statuit. patrimonium omne suum, quod in Macedonia Europaque habebat, amicis dividit, sibi Asiam sufficere praefatus.

Walter is careful to keep Alexander's statement that Asia is enough for him. Indeed, he adds to the emphasis of this theme by making the assertion a direct quote (mihi sufficit una / haec regio). We will see that this passage is but the first of a series of statements which build finally to the topos that the world itself was insufficient for Alexander's ambition.

When Alexander comes to the tomb of Achilles, he is moved to deliver a long speech to his men. It is divided into two parts. The first part concerns Fortuna (1.478-498):

> «o Fortuna viri superexcellentior,» inquit,
> «cuius Maeonium redolent praeconia vatem,
> qui licet exanimem distraxerit Hectora, robur
> et patrem patriae, summum tamen illud honoris
> arbitror augmentum, quod tantum tantus habere
> post obitum meruit praeconem laudis Homerum.
> o utinam nostros resoluto corpore tantis
> laudibus extollat non invida fama triumphos!
> nam cum lata meas susceperit area leges,
> cum domitus Ganges, et cum pessumdatus Atlas,
> cum vires Macetum Boreas, cum senserit Ammon,
> et contentus erit sic solo principe mundus
> ut solo sole, hoc unum mihi deesse timebo,
> post mortem cineri ne desit fama sepulto,
> Elysiisque velim solam hanc praeponere campis.
> nec vos excutiat coepto gens provida bello,
> Argolici, Fortuna licet quandoque minetur
> aspera, quae numquam vultu persistit eodem.
> blanditiis indignus erit mollique potiri
> Fortuna, qui dura pati vel amara recusat:
> nam quae dura prius fuerant mollescere vidi.

Alexander's opening exclamation is the first explicit mention of Fortuna in the epic. The mention, and the importance of Fortuna in Alexander's frame of thought, could hardly be made more emphatic. In Alexander's mind, Fortuna and glory (praeconia) are linked. He envies the glory which the *Iliad* brought to Achilles, and desires his own herald of praise (praeconem laudis) to spread his name. Indeed, a lack of fame after his death (post mortem...ne desit fama) is Alexander's only fear; and we are reminded that it is precisely such *fama* that Aristotle held out to his pupil as the natural result of *virtus*. On the other hand, we have seen that the *Consolation* contains a statement on the futility of the hope that any writer can grant true fame. Goaded by his desire for glory, nevertheless, Alexander urges his men not to desist from the war which they have just begun. To encourage them against losing heart in times of hardship, he reminds them of Fortuna's fickle nature (quae numquam vultu persistit eodem); but with this admission, of course, he reaffirms the notion of the instability of secular affairs (19).

The second part of Alexander's speech (1.499-538) recounts a dream which has given him confidence of success despite his expressed knowledge of the changing face of Fortuna (1.500: unde haec tanta meae surgat fiducia menti) (20). The immediate source of this tale—the miraculous appearance to Alexander of the High Priest of Jerusalem—is Josephus, or rather a Latin epitome of his *Antiquitates*. But Walter has made significant changes in the story which he received. The first of these changes is to make the recounting of the vision a part of Alexander's speech at the tomb of Achilles, thus tying it more closely to the themes of Alexander's thirst for glory and of the role of Fortuna in human affairs. Walter also adds a description of Alexander's emotional state at the time of the vision (1.504-515):

---

(19) Malkiel's study of the theme of glory in the *Alexandreis* (*op. cit.*, pp. 128-135) is inadequate and misleading. In order to argue that Walter is extolling glory as a goal of heroic activity, she separates the references to the *Consolation* which she notices from the main body of her chapter. Interestingly, her interpretation of the theme of glory in the *Libro de Alexandre* has been attacked by Ian Michael, *The Treatment of Classical Material in the «Libro de Alexandre»* (Manchester, 1970), pp. 278-280, as ignoring the poet's criticism of Alexander.

(20) Walter may have taken his assumption of Alexander's trust in Fortuna from Curtius 7.9.1.

nocte fere media, somnum suadentibus astris,
pulvinar regale premens penetralibus altis
solus eram: socios laxabat inertia somni,
at mea pervigiles urebant pectora curae:
cumque super regni ratio novitate labaret,
incertus, hostes sequerer, patriamve tuerer,
in neutro stabilis, facturus utrumque videbar.
ecce locum subita radiantem lampade vidi,
et coeleste iubar noctis caligine pressa
irrupisse fores, tenebrasque diescere vidi:
cum timor incuteret mentem, testemque pavoris
sentirem trepidos sudorem errare per artus.

It is the middle of the night. Alexander is alone, unable to sleep, beset by cares and doubts. Then he is frightened (cum timor incuteret mentem) by the sudden appearance of a man in foreign garb who promises to him ultimate victory in his quest for world domination in return for sparing «my people,» and disappears (1.532-536):

«egredere, o Macedo fortissime, finibus,» inquit,
«a patriis, omnemque tibi pessumdabo terram.
at si me tibi forte vides occurrere talem,
parce meis,» dixit, superasque recessit in auras,
discedensque domum miro perfudit odore.

By his changes Walter makes the scene conform to a common pattern of literary dream visions; in addition, his language reflects the attempt to evoke simultaneously three specific models—the *Aeneid, Bellum Civile* and *Consolation*—and through such evocation to invest the scene with greater meaning.

There are four visions in the *Bellum Civile*. This first vision of Walter's epic draws on the first in Lucan's. Caesar, on reaching the banks of the Rubicon, sees a vision of Rome herself (1.185-203). The situations of the two conquerors differ: While the High Priest promises victory to Alexander, Rome attempts to dissuade Caesar. Each man is frightened at first, but this response is attributable more to tradition than to conscious modelling. More important, each scene is used to provide a context for expressing the leader's confidence in his Fortuna. For Alexander, the vision proves that Fortuna, though by her nature unstable, favors him. Caesar, on the other hand, rejects Rome's warning (1.223-227):

> Caesar, ut adversam superato gurgite ripam
> attigit, Hesperiae vetitis et constitit arvis,
> «hic,» ait «hic pacem temerataque iura relinquo;
> te, Fortuna, sequor. procul hinc iam foedera sunto;
> credidimus satis his, utendum est iudice bello.»

After crossing the Rubicon, he exclaims his intention to «follow Fortuna» (te, Fortuna, sequor). This is the first mention of Fortuna in the *Bellum Civile,* just as the speech in which Alexander describes his vision contains the first explicit mention of Fortuna in the *Alexandreis.* Later, Lucan makes a statement explaining what Fortuna means to Caesar (7.796: Fortunam superosque suos in sanguine cernit). This definition can also, I think, be applied to the understanding of Fortuna by the Alexander of Walter's epic.

Now the *Aeneid.* The vanishing of the High Priest from Alexander's sight contains in the phrase *superasque recessit in auras* an unmistakable allusion to Creusa's departure from Aeneas after her *imago* appears to him in Troy (*Aeneid* 2.790-791):

> haec ubi dicta dedit, lacrimantem et multa volentem
> dicere deseruit, tenuisque recessit in auras.

This allusion is most suggestive. The words of Creusa remove from Aeneas much of his indecision about leaving Troy. In like manner, the promise of the High Priest gives the wavering Alexander the confidence to depart for Asia.

The theme of indecision ties the vision of Alexander even more suggestively to the *Consolation.* Alexander's description of himself as *in neutro stabilis* is the third reference to «stability» in the epic. Aristotle had warned that avarice can undermine the rational control (mentem stabilem) which is a essential component of *virtus*; then Cleadas had warned against the instability of a kingdom ruled without *clementia*. Both these earlier statements have a connection with the theme of Fortuna. The stable mind, Aristotle suggests, should not be affected by the vicissitudes of experience; and I have already noted that Philosophy's argument is predicated on the assumption that there can be no *regnum stabile* on earth. Moreover, Alexander's indecision is directly tied to Fortuna; for he mentions it at the beginning of his explanation of his confidence despite his knowledge of the mutable affections of luck. The vision of the High Priest, as Alexander tells it, links him to Boethius. Each man, distraught, receives a visit from someone in strange garb who will resolve his concern about his present state. A verbal allusion enhances this similarity. Boethius cannot at first identify Philosophy because his vision is clouded by tears (1. pr. 1: ego cuius acies mersa caligaret). Alexander beholds the High Priest when a sudden light disperses the clouds of night (noctis caligine pressa).

This complex of allusions to three other works—the *Bellum Civile, Aeneid* and *Consolation*—suggests at least two very different lines of thematic development available to Walter. Does Alexander's vision, like the visit of Philosophy to Boethius, mark the beginning of an epic journey toward *beatitudo*? If so, then Walter's goal would seem to be an integration of the moral and physical quests, much as we now realize Vergil adds a moral dimension to the wanderings of Odysseus. The corresponding visions of Aeneas and even Caesar, after all, both occur at critical moments of hesitation. Rome's plea cannot dissuade Caesar from the fateful act of crossing the Rubicon, while Creusa's words help dissolve the unwillingness of Aeneas to leave Troy. Conversely, Walter has before him the possibility of using the *Consolation* as the basis for an attack on the imperfect journey, as he understands it, of a hero like Aeneas toward worldly success without spiritual enlightenment. Alexander may embark on a series of conquests which will bring the world at his feet but not the intellectual growth attained by Boethius inside his jail cell. In either case, Walter's decision will be reflected in his handling of the themes of *gloria* and Fortuna.

Having established the importance of these two themes in Book One, in Book Two Walter develops them with specific reference to the careers of Alexander and Darius. Our attention is directed first to the former, then to the latter as they move inexorably toward a confrontation at Issus. First, Alexander. In Book Two the Macedonian, who has talked about the variability of human life (1.494-498), now experiences it for the first time when he decides to go swimming (2.148-154):

> purus et illimis mediam perlabitur urbem
> Cydnus, qui gelidos haurit de fontibus amnes,
> contentus sese est, nullasque aliunde ruentis
> admittit torrentis aquas, sed gurgite ludit
> calculus, et refluo lapsu lascivit arena.
> hic primum didicit Magnus durare salutem
> nulli continuam, sed mixta adversa secundis.

While swimming in the cold waters of the Cydnus, Alexander suddenly is stricken seriously ill. After he is dragged unconscious to the bank, the Greek army pours out its grief—to Fortuna (2.173-185):

> flos iuvenum Macedo, quis te impetus inter amicos
> nudum, quis casus inopina morte subegit?
> improba, mobilior folio Fortuna caduco,
> tigribus asperior, diris immitior hydris,
> Tisiphone horridior, monstro truculentior omni,
> cur metis ante diem florentes principis annos?
> hactenus exstiteras mater, quis te impulit illi
> velle novercari, quem promissum sibi regem
> mundus adoptabat? sed quis manet exitus illos,
> optime rex, quibus a patria tua castra secutis
> non licet in patriam loca per deserta reverti?
> numquid nos sine te medios mittemur in hostes?
> sed quis dignus erit tanto succedere regi?

Fortuna is more fickle than a leaf, harsher than a tiger, the most horrible of all monsters because she has taken Alexander from them. They are concerned for him, and for themselves. Who will lead them now that they are stranded in Asia?

Fortuna chances to hear this complaint while she sits turning her wheel (2.186: rotam volvendo). This picture, with its allusion to the *Consolation* (2. pr. 3: rotam volubili orbe versamus) (21), prepares us for Fortuna's own statement on her behalf (2.190-200):

> inscia mens hominum quanta caligine fati
> pressa iacet, quae me toties iniusta lacessit!
> ius reliquis proprium licet exercere deabus,
> me solam excipiunt: quae dum bona confero magnis
> laudibus attollor, sed quando retraxero rebus
> imperiosa manum rea criminis arguor, ac si
> naturae stabilis sub conditione teneri
> possem: si semper apud omnes una manerem
> aut eadem, iam non merito Fortuna vocarer.
> lex mihi natura posita est sine lege moveri,
> solaque mobilitas stabilem facit.

By this speech Walter is without question tying the Fortuna of the *Alexandreis* to her counterpart in the *Consolation*. The argument of her reply is modelled on Fortuna's long self-defense in *Consolation* 2. pr. 2. The verbal echo of *quando retraxero...manum* (cf. 2. pr. 2: nunc mihi retrahere manum libet) enhances that resemblance. Walter seems also to have had in mind the following passage from the *Consolation* (2. pr. 1):

> quid est igitur o homo quod te in maestitiam luctumque deiecit? novum, credo, aliquid inusitatumque vidisti. tu Fortunam putas erga te esse mutatam;

---

(21) Note Walter's foreshadowing of this phrase at 2.38-39:
forma rotunda pilae sphaeram speciemque rotundi,
quem mihi subiiciam, pulchre determinat orbis.

> erras. hi semper eius mores sunt ista natura. servavit circa te propriam potius in ipsa sui mutabilitate constantiam. talis erat cum blandiebatur, cum tibi falsae inlecebris felicitatis alluderet. deprehendisti caeci numinis ambiguos vultus.

The speaker is Philosophy, her argument that one should not complain because Fortuna is acting according to her nature. Here too Fortuna is blind; and the oxymoron of *mutabilitate constantiam* in this passage may have provided the model for Walter's play on *mobilitas stabilem* at the end of his own passage.

The prominence of Fortuna in this scene is Walter's invention. The general line of the narrative follows Curtius' account (3.5-6...17); but the lament of the soldiers as given by Curtius makes no mention of Fortuna. She is referred to only in passing by Alexander after he recovers consciousness and demands a physician (3.5.11: «in quo me,» inquit, «articulo rerum mearum Fortuna deprehenderit, cernitis»). Not only does Walter make Fortuna the subject of the soldiers' lament but even changes the description of the waters of the Cydnus to foreshadow her importance in the scene. Curtius had merely described the clarity and gentle course of the frigid waters; but he makes no mention of the playful eddies and frolicking sands (gurgite ludit / calculus, et refluo lapsu lascivit arena) which Walter emphasizes in the last line of his description. But of course the idea of play (ludit) invites thoughts of Fortuna. Alexander is learning of her fickleness (nulli continuam) more than about health; and the soldiers are correct in directing their dismay to her. Moreover, Walter also introduces into his scene the companion theme of glory. In Curtius Alexander says that he is unwilling to die an obscure and ignoble death (2.5.10: obscuraque et ignobili morte). Walter is more specific. Alexander demands to be cured lest he die *inglorius* (2.219) and *sine laude* (2.220).

After the recovery of Alexander, the narrative turns to Darius; but Fortuna continues to occupy center stage. Darius receives good advice (2.286: utile consilium), which he rejects, to divide his treasure on the chance that Fortuna favor the Greeks in the first encounter (2.281-282: si Fortuna, quod absit, / faverit Argolicis). This connection of war with Fortuna is strengthened when Thymodas, in presenting a plan of attack, argues (2.284-285).

> non mediocris enim furor est exponere bellis
> uno velle simul Fortunae cuncta sub ictu.

Darius' reply continues the now well established linking of the themes of Fortuna and glory. It may be madness to risk all, he says, but to proceed otherwise would bring him shame (2.295: dedecus) and ill repute (2.297: saeva infamia).

Darius decides, instead, to meet Alexander in a pitched battle; and in a speech which parallels Alexander's address to his troops in Book One, he tries to lift the spirits of his men (2.325-371). This speech, like Alexander's, is divided into two parts. The first part (2.325-353) deals primarily with glory and Fortuna; the second part (2.354-371) describes a confidence inspiring dream. Darius begins by calling Alexander «that illegitimate boy» (2.333: spurius ille puer), and urges the Persians to remember their own proud heritage (2.342-347):

> scire velim, Macedo, quibus inspirante Megaera
> artibus illius Cyri te posse potiri
> imperio iactas, cui Lydia, Croesus et omnes
> curvavere genu quocumque sub axe tyranni,
> qui licet extinctus me successore superstes
> regnat et in vivo vivit Fortuna sepulti.

But Darius' words carry an unintentionally ironic undertone for the reader familiar with the *Consolation*. His emphasis is upon the superiority which the Persians derive from their past greatness (2.357: monumenta priorum) and from his own inheritance of the Fortuna of Cyrus. Boethius, however, attacks the very notion of inherited glory (6. pr. 2: quare splendidum te, si tuam non habes, aliena claritudo non efficit). Moreover, in her *apologia* Fortuna provides an alternate meaning for the *exemplum* of Cyrus and Croesus. Her point, quite naturally, is the inconstancy of human affairs (2. pr. 2):

> an tu mores ignorabas meos? nesciebas Croesum regem Lydorum Cyro paulo ante formidabilem mox deinde miserandum rogi flammis traditum misso caelitus imbre defensum?... quid tragoediarum clamor aliud deflet nisi indiscreto ictu Fortunam felicia regna vertentem?

Croesus, once a terror to Cyrus, was rendered pitiable (miserandum). Fortuna overturns happy conditions with an impartial blow (indiscreto ictu). And this reference to the *ictus Fortunae* takes us back to Thymodas' unheeded warning against placing too much confidence *sub ictu Fortunae*.

As did Alexander, Darius now recounts a dream to explain his confident anticipation of victory. The vision is deceptive. Curtius' version of the event includes the pessimistic interpretations of some of Darius' counsellors (3.3.2-7). Walter omits these, but adds an apostrophe to the Persian soldiers (2.381: quo ruitis peritura manus?) as they head toward defeat.

Walter builds to the battle itself by directing our attention alternately to Alexander and Darius. A simile comparing Alexander to a wolf (2.398-407) reminds us that the Macedonian has indeed reached maturity. Then we see Darius deploying his forces (2.414-421):

> Darius tamen, agmine rursus
> disposito, caute secum deliberat hostem
> milite consulto vi circumcingere multa.
> utile propositum regique suisque salubre,
> quod ratus est, verum ratione potentior omni
> discussit Fortuna procax, quae sola tuetur
> tuta, gravata levat, cassat rata, foedera rumpit,
> infirmat firmum, fixum movet, ardua frangit.

The idea is taken from Curtius (3.8.30: ceterum destinata salubriter omni ratione potentior Fortuna discussit). But the *amplificatio* is Walter's. Fortuna is more than powerful; she is in essence the protagonist here. Walter then emphasizes the unfortunate state of her plaything Darius with two punning references to the «stability» (2.422: stabilita... 424: stabilem peditum...vallum) of the opposing force.

Alexander now addresses his army (2.450-486). Not unexpectedly he begins with Fortuna and ends with glory. Fortuna, he announces, has prepared the way for victory (2.450-456):

> martia progenies, quorum ditione teneri,
> legibus adstringi totus desiderat orbis,
> ecce dies optata, parat qua provida nobis
> solvere promissum toties Fortuna triumphum,
> cuius in Europa dudum praeludia gessi,
> cum genus Aonidum totamque a sedibus urbem
> delestis, soloque metu domuistis Athenas.

Alexander's trust in Fortuna remains firm (provida...Fortuna); and after exhorting the men to fight cruelly and without mercy, he concludes (2.484-486):

> proelia non spolium mecum discernite, cedant
> praemia, praeda meis, mihi gloria sufficit una:
> rem vobis, mihi nomen amo.

Another of Walter's additions, this is Alexander's second statement of what is «enough» for him (cf. 1.440-441). His sole concern is fame. Glory alone suffices (mihi gloria sufficit una). Alexander loves his name (mihi nomen amo), that is, the extension of his name *per saecula*.

The final line of Alexander's speech blends into what appears to be the beginning of the battle (2.486-496):

>   sic fatur, et ecce
> concurrunt acies: Persae clamore soluto
> horrisonis vexant tenues ululatibus auras,
> classica terrifico destringunt arva boatu.

> hinc fit et inde sonus, lituis eliditur aer,
> et referunt raucos montana cacumina cantus,
> quaeque sonos iterat purum sine corpore nomen
> responsura fuit numquam tot vocibus echo.

Walter devotes seven lines to various noise topoi, ending with a learned mythological allusion to Echo. He then seems to turn to the topos of the glitter of the weapons (2.494-495):

> arma tamen Darii multo sudore fabrili
> parta micant, referuntque virum monumenta
> [priorum.

Instead, Walter interrupts the flow of the narrative to give a lengthy *ekphrasis* devoted to the shield of Darius (2.497-539). Such a digression is, to be sure, a conventional feature of epic (22). But this fact does not explain why Walter inserts the *descriptio* here or his apparent awkwardness in doing so. I suggest that the suddenness of the transition is for emphasis, and that Walter places the passage at the conclusion of Book Two so that its content can reinforce the meaning of what has gone before. On the shield is depicted the entire history of the Persians; but all else is literally circumscribed by the accomplishments of Cyrus (2.526-529):

> sed totum circuit orbem
> atque oras ambit clipei celeberrima Cyri
> historia; a tanto superari principe gaudet
> Lydia et ambiguo deceptus Apolllline Croesus.

We meet again the story of Cyrus and Croesus to which Darius made reference in his speech (2.342-347). There the theme of the inconstancy of glory was only implied by the reference to Cyrus' Fortuna. Now Walter makes his intention clear by using this *exemplum* to explain the point of the *ekphrasis* (2.533-539):

---

(22) See the comment by Raby, *op. cit.* II, p. 74.

> proh gloria fallax
> imperii, proh quanta patent ludibria sortis
> humanae! Cyrum terrae pelagique potentem,
> delicias orbis, quem summo culmine rerum
> extulerat virtus, quem fama locarat in astris,
> qui rector composque sui, qui totus et unus
> malleus orbis erat, imbellis femina fregit.

Earlier Walter used Cyrus' defeat of Croesus as an *exemplum* of the inevitable alternation of success and failure in human life. Cyrus too, raised to a pinnacle by *virtus,* had to fall. As his story encircles the shield, so his life reflects the wheel of Fortuna. The mention of Cyrus both concludes the digession and provokes Walter's exclamation. The language of that exclamation—indeed the very notion of an exclamation—was inspired by the words of Philosophy in the *Consolation* (3. pr. 6: gloria vero quam fallax saepe, quam turpis est!). The glory for which Darius and Alexander are striving is a fleeting thing. Walter has interrupted the battle scene to make that point.

In Book Two, then, Walter both sets the scene for the battle of Issus and denigrates its importance. The allusions to the *Consolation* in Fortuna's *apologia* point to a Boethian inspiration for her portrait in the *Alexandreis*. Other reminiscences of the *Consolation* are used to cast the quest for *gloria* in a wholly negative light. At the same time Walter emphasizes the desire of both Alexander and Darius to gain the very kind of fame which is dismissed as *vanitas*. As they rush to battle, they are shown to be fighting for a transient and ultimately unimportant prize.

The action of Book Three contrasts the situations of the two antagonists in a way which illustrates the paradox, articulated by Philosophy in the *Consolation,* that Fortuna when adverse is more profitable to men than when she is favorable (2. pr. 8: etenim plus hominibus reor adversam quam prosperam prodesse Fortunam). The narrative reveals the two heroes on the wheel of Fortuna. In begins with the defeat of Darius and the capture of his wife and son. Yet by the last lines a «greater Darius» (arg. 3.7-8: Darius reparato robore rursus /

maior) has emerged, while the victor Alexander is bedeviled by sedition.

At the beginning of the book, Alexander seems enviable in every respect. His army wins the battle. He himself shows not only courage but also incredible restraint. When he is attacked by the seer Zoroas, he even allows himself to be wounded in the thigh before he is forced to kill him (3.140-188). After the battle, Walter sharply contrasts the brutal actions of the soldiers (3.225-233) with Alexander's *clementia* (3.236: tanta est clementia regis) and love of *virtus* (3.241-242: tantus enim virtutis amor tunc temporis illi / pectore regnabat). But life on the wheel is hardly secure. In mid-line Walter shifts to a prediction of Alexander's fall—not from success, but from *virtus* (3.242-244):

> si perdurasset in illo
> ille tenor, non est quo denigrare valeret
> crimine candentem titulis infamia famam.

This statement contains an interesting interplay of ideas. Walter says that Alexander's fame would have been unsullied had he endured in his noble behavior; and yet fame is associated with Fortuna, and in the realm of Fortuna nothing can stay the same. The following lines continue to lament Alexander's eventual decline, and Walter seems to follow Curtius in attributing that moral decay to the influence of Fortuna (3.248: corrupit Fortuna physim); for his success had brought Alexander «wealth, the begetter of luxury» (3.247: genetrix opulentia luxus)—these words being a recollection of Aristotle's warning against the corrupting power of *avaritia* and *luxuries*.

Unexpectedly we now learn that Darius, though defeated, has in the workings of Fortuna a *medicina mali* (3.272). I refer to the death of the traitorous governor of Damascus. Walter repeats the notion found in Curtius (3.13.17: opportunum solacium) that the destruction of this man was a solace for Darius (3.266-267: Dario solamen id unum / ...fuit); but he adds to his version a lesson concerning Fortuna (3.266-273):

> Dario solamen id unum
> damnorum luctusque fuit, cum nuntius ipsum
> artificem sceleris afferret in agmine primo
> arte perisse sua, nec iniquam sustinet ultra
> dicere Fortunam, quae iusta lance rependit
> sontibus interdum, prout fraus ignava meretur.
> haec Dario medicina mali: sic paene malorum
> omnia cum quodam veniunt incommoda fructu.

The death of the traitor teaches Darius not to label Fortuna «unfair» (iniquam); for her impartial, or better amoral, mingling of success and failure results occasionally in a balancing of the scales. There is some compensation along with almost all evils (sic paene malorum / omnia cum quodam veniunt incommoda fructu). Thus Darius in failure gains a degree of understanding concerning the workings of Fortuna and even solace from that understanding, while the successful Alexander begins a plunge into vice (3.249: vitiorum cautibus haerens) because of Fortuna's favor. In this respect we can see in the contrast drawn between the two at the beginning of Book Three an evocation of the Boethian paradox.

Three other references to Fortuna in this book emphasize further her contribution to Alexander's military success; at the same time, they recall the instability of such favor by foreshadowing his death. First, during the siege of Gaza an attempt by the populace to resist Fortuna (3.347: Fortuna... evertere) by killing Alexander fails. This failure Walter attributes to the immovable order of the Fates (3.352-353: fatorum...inevitabilis ordo... / series immobilis); but his point is that they are preserving him only for a different death ten years later (3.354-358):

> erravit tremulenta manus, ferroque perire
> non patitur Lachesis, cui iam fatale venenum
> confectumque diu lethea faece vitrina
> pyxide condierat mediante favore suorum
> porrectura duci dea post duo lustra bibendum.

It is of interest to note here that Walter, like Gerald in the

Waltharius, seems intent upon keeping the ending of his epic in our minds. Now we know that poison will be the means of Alexander's murder.

The second of the three references is to the attempt of Darius to deflect the course of Fortuna (3.441: Fortunae flectere cursum), that is, defeat Alexander; but again his plan is to be foiled by Alexander's luck (3.448-449: sorte secunda / usus Alexander). The third reference to Fortuna occurs after the opposing armies have pitched camp. An eclipse of the moon frightens Alexander's men, who are moved to the point of rebellion (3.489-495). Walter introduces into his account of this episode, which otherwise follows Curtius (4.10.1-12) rather closely, a speech by the soothsayer Aristander (3.501-538). His opening words (3.503: parcite, ait, vanis incessere fata querelis) echo the beginning of Fortuna's *apologia* in the *Consolation* (2. pr. 2: quid tu homo ream me cotidianis agis querelis?). He goes on to explain the eclipse as merely a natural event which follows discernible laws. At the end of Aristander's discourse Walter places another reference to Fortuna missing in Curtius' version (3.526-529):

> dixit et exemplis veterum pro teste revolvit
> Persidis acta ducum, quibus incumbente flagello
> Fortunae obscuro lugubris Cynthia cornu
> palluerat.

These added allusions to Fortuna make the scene all the more effective by building on the common association of the waxing and waning moon with Fortuna (cf. *Carmina Burana* 14.1: o Fortuna velut luna). They also give added significance to the description of the army—taken from Curtius—after it is convinced by Aristander's words (3.529-537):

> stetit ergo ratum, quod cana senectus
> arguerat, meruitque fidem sententia vatis,
> editaque in medium flexit pavitantia vulgi
> corda superstitio, qua nil adstrictius ad se
> inclinat turbam, regit ora manusque refrenat.

> quae cum saeva, potens, mutabilis, aestuat aestu
> multivagae mentis, vana si forte movetur
> relligione, ducum spreto moderamine, vatum
> imperium subit et regum contemnit habenas.

Walter indicates in this passage the perverse result of Aristander's reasoned argument. His talk of a fixed order to natural occurrences (3.506: *haec certo ordine servant*) has been used to arouse in the soldiers a *superstitio* which renders them more tractable. Alexander takes full advantage of their sudden confidence (3.538: *fiducia fati*) to break camp and set up battle conditions even though it is the middle of the night. As for the men as they commit themselves to follow Alexander, they are a crowd which is *saeva, potens, mutabilis*. In sum, Walter attaches to them adjectives just as descriptive of Fortuna herself. In following Alexander, they follow her.

Book Four offers something of a pause in the flow of the narrative. Much of it is spent describing Alexander's indecision on the eve of the battle of Arbela, which will not take place until the next book. Moreover, we have in this book two long *ekphraseis*—the tomb of Darius' wife and the temple of Victory. There is no interruption, however, in the development of the underlying argument of the epic—that Alexander's devotion to Fortuna and desire for glory prevent him from being a true exemplar of *virtus*. Consider, for example, the treatment by Walter of the aftermath of the death of Darius' wife. The Persian king, moved by reports of the respect which Alexander showed her, makes an offer—sprinkled, to be sure, with threats—of peace and reconciliation. Alexander's angry rejection of that offer contains the expected emphasis on Fortuna and glory (4.131-141):

> consulis arbitrium tulit aegre Magnus, «et a me,
> si essem Parmenion, oblata pecunia palmae
> praeferretur, ait, mallemque inglorius esse,
> quam sine divitiis palmam cum laude mereri.
> at nunc securus sub paupertatis amictu
> regnat Alexander: regem me glorior esse,

> non mercatorem: Fortunae venditor absit.
> nil venale mihi: si reddendos fore constat,
> gratius hos gratis reddi donoque remitti
> censeo quam censu: pretium si dona sequantur,
> gratia non sequitur, nec habent commercia grates.»

Alexander is incensed when Parmenio counsels the acceptance of Darius' offer. Unlike his officer, Alexander is unwilling to do without glory in favor of wealth; for he is a king, not a merchant or «purchaser of Fortuna» (Fortunae venditor absit). But Alexander's proud words include as well a hint of his downfall. When he speaks of reigning securely under the mantle of poverty (nunc securus sub paupertatis amictu), we are reminded both of the insecurity of all earthly power and of the *opulentia* which has been cited as the cause of his slipping into vice.

The episode concludes with the construction and ornamentation of a tomb for Stateira; and on it the Jew Apelles sculpts the events of Old Testament history from the creation of the world to Ezra. These scenes complement the depiction of Persian history on Darius' shield (2.494-539). The one figure who appears in both *ekphraseis* is Cyrus. On the shield, his mention is the cause of Walter's exclamation concerning *gloria fallax*, with emphasis on Cyrus' destruction at the height of his greatness by a woman (2.539: imbellis femina fregit). In the latter *descriptio*, Cyrus is mentioned after Walter provides figural interpretations of events leading to the birth and death of Christ (4.258-268). In contrast to the role of a woman in the demise of Cyrus, here we have emphasis on the role of a woman in the salvation of mankind itself (4.259: virgo concupiet). Implied also in Walter's treatment is a distinction between the secular history depicted on the shield and the events of the Old Testament on the tomb. The former, like Darius and Alexander, is tied to the vicissitudes of Fortuna; the latter is the prelude to something truly great and permanent.

The rest of Book Four, which depicts Alexander's crisis of confidence immediately before the battle of Arbela, establishes the fact that he cannot imagine any force except Fortuna exercising control over his life. Walter has taken what is a relatively minor scene in Curtius and amplified it to give it greater impact and deeper meaning. The heart of Curtius' version is worth citing (4.13.14-17):

> similis apud Macedones quoque sollicitudo erat; noctemque, velut in eam certamine edicto, metu egerunt. Alexander, non alias magis territus, ad vota et preces Aristandrum vocari iubet. ille in candida veste verbenas manu praeferens, capite velato, praeibat preces regi Iovem Minervamque Victoriam propitianti, tunc quidem, sacrificio rite perpetrato, reliquum noctis acquieturus in tabernaculum rediit. sed nec somnum capere nec quietem pati poterat; modo e iugo montis aciem in dextrum Persarum cornu demittere agitabat, modo recta fronte concurrere hosti, interdum haesitare an potius in laevum detorqueret agmen. tandem gravatum animi anxietate corpus altior somnus oppressit. iamque luce orta duces ad accipienda imperia convenerant, insolito circa praetorium silentio attoniti... ad haec Alexander: «credisne me prius somnum capere potuisse quam exonerarem animum sollicitudine quae quietem morabatur?» signumque pugnae tuba dari iussit...haud alias tam alacrem viderant regem et ex vultu eius interrito certam spem victoriae augurabantur.

Uncertain what strategy to employ, Alexander is unable to sleep. When at last he falls asleep, it is an unusually deep slumber. When Parmenio wakes the king, he simply says that he could not rest until he had resolved his doubts. He orders the battle begun; and he looks so confident that the soldiers assume victory to be certain.

Walter's changes in the episode begin with Curtius' comment about Alexander's state of concern, which Walter turns into a declaration that the sight of the two armies struck fear into Alexander's heart (4.313-315):

> quae cuncta viro, si credere fas est,
> incussere metum, facilemque ad nobile pectus
> corque giganteum reor adscendisse pavorem.

He then inserts an extended simile to emphasize not only Alexander's alarm but also the resulting indecision in his mind (4.316-327):

> non alio Tiphys curarum fluctuat aestu,
> cui blandita diu Zephyri moderantia solo
> flamine contentam duxit sine remige puppim,
> Nereidumque chorus placidis epulatur in undis,
> si procul instantes videat fervere procellas,
> et celeres phocas imis a sedibus Auster
> praemittens, madidis iam verberet aera pennis.
> inclamat sociis, laxisque rudentibus ipse
> convolat ad clavam laterique aplustre maritat:
> non secus, ut vidit tot milibus arva prementes
> barbaricos instare globos, iam credere fas est
> magnanimum timuisse ducem.

The image of a storm tossed ship (sine remige puppim) was commonly used to express the notion of a life controlled by the power of Fortuna. One source for this image is, of course, the *Consolation* (2. pr. 2):

> ius est mari nunc strato aequore blandiri, nunc procellis ac fluctibus inhorrescere.

Not surprisingly, the presence of the theme of Fortuna is followed by a reference to glory. Alexander seeks Parmenio's advice; but when that advice turns out to be a night attack, he rejects it (4.353-366):

> hic latronis ait mos et sollertia furum,
> quam mihi suggeritis, quorum spes unica, voti
> summa, nocere dolis et fallere fraude latenti.
> gloria nostra dolo non militet: ut nihil obstet,
> quod mihi candorem famae fuligine labis
> obscurare queat, iam non angustia saltus

> et Cilicum fauces, Dariive absentia segnis,
> nec furtiva placent timidae suffragia noctis.
> aggrediar de luce viros: victoria quam nos
> molimur gladiis aut nulla sit aut sit honesta.
> malo poeniteat Fortunae et sortis iniquae
> regem, quam pudeat parti de nocte triumphi.
> vincere non tanti est, ut me vicisse dolose
> posteritas legat et minuat versutia famam.

Alexander's primary concern is that the glory of his victory not be tarnished by the manner in which he gains it. A night attack will dull the brightness of his reputation (candorem famae...obscurare). And he worries that his Homer will be compelled to write of a victory that will diminish his glory (minuat versutia famam). The reasoning is the same as that which led Alexander to reject Darius' proposal earlier in this book (4.131-141).

The structure of this entire episode bears a strong resemblance to that in Book One at the tomb of Achilles (1.468-538). There too Alexander's indecision was tied closely to his concern for glory; here, as there, that lack of confidence is dissipated by a supernatural agent; for Walter introduces the epic convention of the divine messenger sent to the hero. Victory, seeing Alexander burdened with cares, sends Sleep to give him rest. Her charge to Somnus is preceded by another *ekphrasis*, the description of the temple of Victoria (4.401-432). The sleep sent by Victory renews Alexander's confidence, and his men notice the change in him (4.522-525):

> non magis a primo duri discrimine Martis
> hunc alacrem videre sui: veniente suorum
> in medium Magno, spes sana resuscitat aegrum
> agmen, et in vultu Victoria visa sedere est.

The change from Curtius' wording is effective. Now the reference to Victory is stated in a way that reminds us that she is the source of Alexander's renewed confidence. Fortuna played no part in the event; indeed, the *ekphrasis*, though it catalogues

the many powers which accompany Victory, makes no mention
of her. However, Alexander sees Fortuna alone as the force
operating in his life (4.546-562):

> tunc vero fluentes
> praecedens acies, verbo nutuque loquaci
> ad lites animans: «vestris labor ultimus,» inquit,
> «prae manibus, socii. bellum quod Granicus amnis
> vidit et angusto Cilicum victoria saltu,
> quid laudis, quid honoris habent, nisi fine beato
> terminet extremum deus et Fortuna triumphum?
> ced Fortuna deus ea, quae pro viribus adstans
> semper Alexandro, tam sub me sceptra tenere
> quam sub se gaudet alios regnare potentes.
> haec ubi me Macetum moderantem Graecia vidit
> frena, meos ex tunc promovit, eisque nocere
> velle licet liceat, sed non audere licebit.
> ista nihil praeter numerum discriminis affert
> tam populosa cohors sed ad hoc Fortuna laborat,
> quam pudet exiguos toties numerare triumphos,
> ut mihi vincendum semel et simul offerat orbem.

In this address, which parallels in many respects the exhortation to his troops in Book One, Alexander declares that for him Fortuna is a goddess (Fortuna deus est). Perhaps more important—and certainly more incorrect—is his assertion that she «always» favors him (quae...adstans / semper Alexandro). Both these strong statements concerning Alexander's faith in Fortuna are Walter's invention; they are not to be found in Curtius' version of this address (4.14.1-7). But they are an integral part of the design of the *Alexandreis*. Alexander trusts only in Fortuna; and his trust is based on an assumption of permanence which, as Fortuna herself has stated, is against her nature.

Having reaffirmed his belief in the power of Fortuna, Alexander now reaffirms *gloria* as his motive for action (4.576-583):

> tantum mihi vincite, praedam
> dividite inter vos. qui mecum vincere curas,
> participem me laudis habe, tibi cetera tolle.
> exemplar virtutis habe formamque gerendi
> Martis Alexandrum: nisi primus in agmine primo
> rex apparuerit, si tergum verterit hosti,
> excusatus eris, veniamque merebitur ille
> qui fugiet, qui lentus aget.

The men will gather booty for themselves. Alexander is a participant only in the quest for glory (*participem me laudis habe, tibi cetera tolle*). These, then, are the two dominant characteristics—confidence in Fortuna and a desire for glory—that mark the man who declares himself as an *exemplar virtutis*. For a Christian audience, he seems hardly an appropriate model; and even though to a large degree he meets the definition of *virtus* expounded by Aristotle, his misplaced trust in a steadfast Fortuna undercuts even that degree of heroism, since Walter elsewhere has pointed out, in a passage containing allusions to the wheel, that Alexander's success itself holds the seeds of his downfall. Walter's additions to this scene, in addition to demonstrating his knowledge of the canons of epic imitation, have all served his larger purpose of showing that Alexander is not, as he thinks, an *exemplar virtutis*. He can better be described with the words which Boethius uses with regard to the man who tries to stay the force of Fortuna's ever turning wheel (2. pr. 1: *at omnium mortalium stolidissime, si manere incipit, fors esse desistit*).

Book Five represents the zenith of Alexander's career. Exhibiting extraordinary valor, he leads his army to victory at Arbela. While Darius withdraws into Media, his eventual defeat a certainty, Alexander captures Syria and, at the end of the book, enters Babylon in triumph. It would seem that he well deserves the extravagant praise with which Walter concludes the first half of his epic.

As I noted at the beginning of this chapter, the centerpiece of Walter's description of the battle is the *aristeia* of Alexander, whose confidence in Fortuna seems at this point quite reasonable. When the fighting begins, the Persians mass their attack against him, but his *virtus* and the help of Fortuna keep him safe (5.25: quem duce Fortuna virtus infracta tuetur). The giant Geon is no more successful. He would kill Alexander, *si sineret Fortuna* (5.39), but of course she will allow no such thing. Fortuna does act more in accord with her nature in the case of the Greek Nicanor. His exploits, which I mentioned in passing earlier, at first divert our attention from Alexander, but I think are intended also to remind us that his luck too eventually must turn. Fortuna smiles on his first efforts (5.129-131):

>   primis arrisit subdola gestis
>   eius et excepit blande Fortuna furentem
>   Parmenione satum.

However, the description of Fortuna as *subdola* and the emphasis that she favored Nicanor's *first* deeds lead us rightly to expect an unhappy conclusion. Moreover, there is an ominous undertone even to Walter's depiction of Nicanor at the height of his success (5.145-147):

>   mixta plebe duces pereunt utrimque, sed inter
>   milia tot procerum speciali laude refulgens
>   inclitus emicuit numerosa caede Nicanor.

The reference to him as *inclitus* cannot but call to mind *inclitus ille* Clitus (5.77), whose death in battle was the last event before the appearance of Nicanor in the episode. Now Walter prepares to describe the end of Nicanor's brief moments of glory (5.167-182):

>   sed quos Hyrcania gignit
>   conspicuos in Marte supervenit ala quiritum
>   excedens numerum, inclusumque Nicanora vallo
>   armisonae sepis facta statione coronant.
>   obruitur primo iaculis: strepit aerea cassis
>   glandibus et saxis, tantamque sibi lacer orbis
>   obstupet innasci veterano robore silvam.

> iamque pedes ulnaeque labant mixtoque cruore
> membra lavat sudor: sed mens infractaque virtus
> et princeps animus fracto sub pectore regnant,
> totque lacessitus iaculis et cestibus ille
> murus Alexandri, sed non sine nomine tandem,
> occubuit, multamque sui cum strage ruinam
> Persarum trahit unius damnosa ruina,
> qualis Romulea cecidit cum turris in urbe
> turbine fulmineo vicinas obruit aedes.

Note, however, that Nicanor's death takes us back to Alexander. He is the *murus Alexandri*; moreover, like Alexander earlier in this same book, he is surrounded by a large force of Persians. The allusions to Alexander do not stop here. Each warrior is protected by his *virtus infracta*—with this difference, that Alexander prevails *duce Fortuna* and Nicanor falls. There is, then, a dark side to the similarity; we are reminded again that Fortuna, even as she favors Alexander in a way he thinks permanent, is a fickle goddess.

The digression finished, the narrative returns to Alexander. Mars sends Bellona to dissuade him from his vain pursuit of Darius (5.222-228):

> labere cara soror, Macetumque, i, nuncia regi
> vana spe raperis, Darium qui perdere per te
> nescius affectas: scelus hoc a principe tanto
> amovere dei, nec fas ut dextera mundi
> sceptra tenens madeat iugulo polluta senili.
> altera debetur Dario Fortuna, suorum
> proditione cadet.

Darius is not to die by Alexander's hand; and Alexander is wrong to hope otherwise (vana spe raperis). Nonetheless, Alexander rejects this divine message (5.241-243):

> excutitur saltu Macedo profugamque sequutus
> voce deam: «quocumque venis dea cardine, vanum
> spernimus omen.»

Alexander throws the word *vanum* back at the goddess, then vows that he himself will kill Darius even if he must pursue him into the underworld (5.252-255):

> sed neque si turris Darium septemplice muro
> includat, licet ardenti circumfluus unda
> sulphureis Acheron defendat moenia ripis,
> eripiet Fortuna mihi!

Once again Alexander expresses himself in terms of Fortuna. Even she will not snatch Darius away from him (eripiet Fortuna mihi). Ironically, this passage foreshadows Alexander's death more than that of Darius. For the moment, however, it is enough to point out that Alexander's words reveal him to be wrong about Fortuna in this specific instance and in general *ignarus futuri*. Darius will not die by his hand.

And what of Darius? Defeated again, he can only ponder and derive some small measure of hope from the variability of Fortuna (5.386-421). While Walter otherwise follows Curtius (5.1.3-9) closely in his account of Darius' flight from Arbela, his musings concerning Fortuna are the poet's invention. Walter has Darius begin with a general statement on the inconstancy of human affairs (5.386-390):

> fortuitos toties, inquit, variare tumultus,
> nunc adversa pati, nunc exultare secundis,
> nunc caput incurvare malis, nunc tollere, sortis
> humanae est: humilem sic vidit Lydia Croesum,
> et sic victorem versa vice femina vicit.

Note that Darius includes another reference to the *exemplum* of Cyrus and Croesus. From the impermanence of success which they typify even the defeated can take heart (5.394-397):

> nulla rei novitas pervertere fortia debet
> pectora, cum nulla teneatur lege fidelis
> esse homini Fortuna diu: spes unica victis
> contra victorem rursus sperare triumphum.

Darius is encouraged by the assumption that Fortuna remains favorable to no man for a long time. Specifically, he is confident that the conquering Macedonians will be corrupted by the wealth of the cities which they capture (5.398-403):

> nec dubito, quin victor agros aditurus et urbes
> civibus exhaustas, sed opimis rebus et auro
> confertas, ubi gens avidissima gutture toto,
> visceribus siccis sitiens letale metallum,
> tentabit sedare sitim praedaque recenti
> conceptam satiare famem.

The language of this last statement contains a striking, and significant, image. We first encountered the image of «thirst» applied to the young Alexander's desire to take up arms against Darius (1.30: arma puer sitiens). Now it is used to emphasize the corrupting power of the riches which Alexander has won by those arms (sitiens letale metallum / tentare sedare sitim); for as Darius makes clear, he is speaking not only of the *gens Macedum* but also of its leader (5.411: maior erat Macedo: spoliis vincetur onustus). The defeated king concludes, without convincing his men, that the Persians will profit by following the practice of their ancestors who, when in dire straits, would withdraw to «repair their Fortuna» (5.420: Fortunam reparasse suam).

Alexander's triumphant entry into Babylon, then, follows close upon Darius' prediction of the debilitating influence of wealth upon him. In this context, Walter's lavish description of the splendor of that city takes on an ironic undertone. That context, and what follows immediately in Book Six suggest as well that the *laudatio* at the end of Book Five (5.491-520) is not what it seems to be. Walter begins by repeating his claim at the beginning of the epic that Alexander's achievements beggar those of the greatest Romans. They are beyond the talent of Claudian or even Lucan to express. Thus he concludes (5.510-520):

> si gemitu commota pio votisque suorum
> flebilibus divina daret clementia talem
> Francorum regem, toto radiaret in orbe
> haud mora vera fides, et nostris fracta sub armis
> Parthia baptismo renovari posceret ultro,
> quaeque diu iacuit effusis moenibus alta
> ad nomen Christi Carthago resurgeret, et quas
> sub Carolo meruit Hispania solvere poenas
> exigerent vexilla crucis: gens omnis et omnis
> lingua Iesum caneret, et non invita subiret
> sacrum sub sacro Remorum praesule fontem.

If France had such a king, the whole world would now be Christian. But if we wish to take this intriguing passage literally and believe that Walter really means to extol Alexander, we are left with the awkwardness of his doing so at the moment of Alexander's entrance into the city whose *luxuria* is going to corrupt him. On the other hand, the ironic intent of this praise, suggested by its placement in the narrative, is not difficult to discern; for in this passage Walter is employing a common rhetorical technique of satire, that is, a succession of serious statements undercut by an absurd conclusion (23). So Juvenal's list of the horrors of life at Rome begins with fires and collapsing houses and ends with poets reciting in the month of August (*Satura* 3.6-9). Here the series proceeds from the baptism of Parthia, the resurgence of Carthage, and the return of Spain to the Christian faith—to the ludicrous picture of Walter's presumably astonished patron trying to cope with the arrival of the whole world for baptism at Reims! The tone of this particular passage is consistent with that of the entire narrative. Walter's praise of Alexander is always blunted, most often by the use of allusions to the *Consolation,* but here by the employment of a technique of another Latin

---

(23) On Walter as a satirist, the best discussion is by Charles Witke, *Latin Satire: The Structure of Persuasion* (Leiden, 1970), pp. 233-266.

genre of which Walter was a consummate master. In sum, like Lucan addressing Nero, he is speaking *per ironiam*.

The second half of the *Alexandreis* begins with emphasis on Alexander's decline from *virtus* (arg. 6.1-2: sextus Alexandrum luxu Babylonis et auro / corruptum ostendit). The first lines of the book, to be sure, seem a continuation of the *laudatio* from Book Five; but a contrary-to-fact clause within the body of the passage suggests that Alexander, having reached his zenith, is about to begin a descent (6.8-15).

> rex erit ille tuus, a quo se posceret omnis
> rege regi tellus, si perdurasset in illa
> indole virtutum, qua coeperat ire potestas.
> adspice quam blandis victos moderetur habenis,
> adspice quam clemens inter tot prospera victor,
> adspice quam mitis dictet ius gentibus, ut quos
> hostes in bellis habuit cognoscat in urbe
> cives, in bello quos vicit vincat amore.

But the prediction of Alexander's decline from *virtus* (si perdurasset in illa / indole virtutum) is followed by a strong three-part statement of his current excellence as a ruler. The list indicates that he has accepted Aristotle's exhortation to *clementia* (adspice quam clemens). I would add that the whole passage is reminiscent of an earlier interjection (3.234-249) in which praise for Alexander's *clementia* is followed immediately by a lament that he would prove incapable of sustaining this high level of conduct. Walter connects the two passages by repeating the use of a contrary-to-fact clause (cf. 3.242-243: si perdurasset in illo / ille tenor) and by suggesting that *luxuria* (3.247: genetrix opulentia luxus) is the seed of his destruction. Such emphasis implies that Walter intends to follow Curtius in examining the deleterious effects of constant good luck on the character of his hero.

Let us return to the analysis of Book Six. Aristotle's advice had included a warning against the corrupting power of *luxuria,* drunkenness, and sexual attraction (1.164-174); and it is precisely the combination of these three vices which, Walter informs us, begins the destruction of Alexander's inborn excellence and the effects of his education (6.16-23):

> hos tamen a tenero schola quos impresserat aevo
> ornatus animi, poliendae schemata vitae,
> innatae virtutis opus solitumque rigorem
> fregerunt Babylonis opes luxusque vacantis
> desidiae populi: quia nil corruptius urbis
> moribus illius, nihil est instructius illis
> ad Veneris venale malum, cum pectora multo
> incaluere mero.

Not that the decay is immediately visible: to the contrary, Alexander treats the defeated Madates with *clementia* and *pietas* (6.135-141). With regard to Fortuna, on the other hand, we can observe a change in Alexander's condition. Walter reintroduces the theme of Fortuna while praising Alexander's actions toward Madates (6.142-144):

> si vaga victori Dario Fortuna dedisset
> urbem prae manibus, non impetrasset ab illo
> plura parens, quam quae victis dedit hostibus hostis.

This reference to inconstant Fortuna (vaga...Fortuna) is not found in Curtius (5.3.5-15), whom this episode otherwise follows. In like manner Walter inserts a reference to Fortuna at the beginnig of his account of the siege of Persepolis (6.150-152):

> non alias Macedo graviosa pericula passus
> experto didicit semper variamque sibique
> dissimilem et nulli Fortunam stare perennem.

Curtius merely says that Alexander's luck came to a standstill (5.3.22: tunc haesitabat deprehensa felicitas). The significance of Walter's change lies in the way the language serves to contradict Alexander's assertion at the end of Book Four (4.553-555) that Fortuna always favors him. Walter's word order stresses that change is Fortuna's only constancy (semper variamque); and he states plainly (nulli Fortunam stare perennem) in language evoking Alexander's own words (4.554-555: adstans / semper Alexandro) that the Macedonian was wrong: Fortuna stands permanently by no man.

Although in the rest of Book Six Walter focuses on other characters, he continues to explore the theme of Fortuna. Following Curtius (5.5.8-21), he includes the debate of the mutilated Greek prisoners at Persepolis as to whether they should now return home or stay in Asia (6.196-296). Walter expands his model, giving more emphasis to Fortuna in the speeches of Euctemon and Theseus (Theaetetus in Curtius). One change in the language of Euctemon's argument deserves special note. In Curtius' version, he simply says that it is no marvel if «the fortunate always seek those like themselves» (5.5.12: quid mirum et fortunatos semper parem quaerere). Walter transforms this into «a lucky roll [of the dice] is accustomed to seek its like» (6.244: fortunata parem solet alea quaerere casum), thus picking up the gambling image of Aristotle's speech which will play an increasingly important role in the epic. To Theseus' speech Walter adds the assertion that «no pious man cares about the mockeries of cruel luck» (6.255-256): durae ludibria sortis / nemo pius pensat). The following also is Walter's invention (6.281-282):

> exsulibus tandem Fortunaeque ultima passis
> est aliquid patrio se reddere posse sepulcro.

It is something at least for those who have suffered the worst of Fortuna to return to the tombs of their fathers. With these additions and changes Walter gives greater emphasis to the contrast between the wretches who have experienced the cruelest blows of Fortuna and the man who has long been her favorite.

Breaking with his source, which now describes the destruction of Persepolis, Walter instead shifts the narrative to another man who knows first hand the mutability of Fortuna. Darius, having decided that he prefers death in battle to prolonging a life of defeat, once again addresses his men (6.312-369). Not only this speech but also the rest of Book Six—the plot of Bessus and Nabarzanes to betray Darius, and the loyalty of his Greek mercenary Patron—follow Curtius closely. Walter makes only two changes worth noting. The first is minor, an expansion of Curtius' expression of the glory which Patron would have gained had Darius taken his advice (5.11.9: Patron quidem egregiam conservati regis gloriam tulerat). In the *Alexandreis* this becomes (6.506-510):

> inclita Patronem servandi gloria regis
> fecerat insignem: si quis tamen haec quoque, si quis
> carmina nostra legat, numquam Patrona tacebit
> Gallica posteritas: vivet cum vate superstes
> gloria Patronis nullum moritura per aevum.

For Walter, this topos has its origin in the *Bellum Civile* (9.980-986), where Lucan speaks of the task of the poet (980: o sacer et magnus vatum labor) and foretells the immortality of his subject (985-986: Pharsalia nostra / vivet et a nullo tenebris damnabimur aevo). The claim by Walter that his poetry can impart a «permanent» glory (gloria...nullum moritura per aevum) to the subjects about whom he writes will appear three times in the *Alexandreis*. Other than making a passing comment on the impossibility (in Boethian terms) of the claim, I must defer for now a discussion of the relation of this passage to the whole theme of glory in the epic.

The second change is of major importance. It occurs as part of Walter's imitation of the statement on the role of chance in human affairs which Curtius interjects into his account of Darius' death. Curtius' argument deserves to be quoted (5.11.10):

> eludant fidem licet quibus forte temere humana negotia agique persuasum est nexuve causarum latentium et multo ante destinatarum suum quemque ordinem immutabili lege percurrere.

Those who ascribe historical events to no force beyond mere chance (forte temere humana negotia volvi agique), he says, will scoff at the assumption that there exists a combination of hidden causes which rules our lives by an immutable law. Curtius then comments that whatever view one holds Darius «at any rate» (certe) sealed his doom by deciding to remain among his own men (5.11.11: quidquid fors tulisset, inter suos perpeti malle quam transfugam fieri). The corresponding argument in the *Alexandreis* concerning the governance of human affairs has a different tone (6.511-515):

> iam reor aeterno causarum saecula nexu
> non temere volvi: nemo temeraria credat
> fortuitoque geri mundana negotia casu:
> omnia lege meant, quam rerum conditor ille
> sanxit ab aeterno.

Walter to be sure makes obvious verbal allusions to the Curtius passage. I can cite *temere volvi, causarum...nexu,* and *mundana* (for *humana*) *negotia* as examples. But Walter's departures from his model are equally obvious. First, in contrast to Curtius' equivocal stance, Walter states his firm belief that events do not occur haphazardly (iam reor...nemo...credat). Second, he introduces a reference to the Christian God (rerum conditor ille) as the originator of the eternal *lex* by which events are ordered. Finally, he rewords the passage to work in pertinent references to the following section of the *Consolation* (1. pr. 6):

> tum illa: «huncine,» inquit, «mundum temerariis agi fortuitisque casibus putas, an ullum credis ei regimen inesse rationis?» «atqui,» inquam, «nullo existimaverim modo ut fortuita temeritate tam certa moveantur, verum operi suo conditorem praesidere deum scio nec umquam fuerit dies qui me ab hac sententiae veritate depellat.

The first sentence, uttered by Philosophy, provides the phrase *fortuitis casibus* which is reflected in Walter's *fortuitoque... casu*. Moreover, Walter's use of *temeraria* (in addition to *temere*, taken from Curtius, in the same line) is an allusion to Boethius' *temerariis...casibus*. Perhaps Walter's *nemo credat* also is a reminiscence of *an...credis* in the *Consolation*. Finally, we see in the Boethian passage a likely model for Walter's reference to God (conditorem praesidere deum). At any rate, the Boethian echoes are consistent with the affirmative, Christian tenor of the argument. What is in Curtius' narrative a brief parenthetical comment is made by Walter an integral part of his deeper theme. For Walter is here developing a Christian context in which one can recognize the illusory nature of the power of Fortuna, who can affect only those who cannot perceive the true order behind her apparent workings. That is, of course, a perception unavailable to the non-Christian Alexander.

In Book Seven, Walter continues what I can now with confidence label his method of adapting his historical sources. His additions and alterations are primarily if not exclusively in the service of his treatment of Fortuna, glory, and their place in the inadequate «heroic» attitude of Alexander. In this book Walter's main departures from Curtius are the invention of a long soliloquy by Darius and an apostrophe concerning greed, which Walter inserts after the death of the Persian king. Where Curtius' narrative breaks off, Walter follows the account given by Justin; but here again Walter adds to what he found, in this case a speech by Alexander and a description of Darius' tomb.

Walter alters Curtius' narrative in order to have Darius again meditate upon the vicissitudes of his life (7.17-58). The point of his speech is that he has not deserved his present misfortune (7.17-20):

> et tamen haec secum: «quos me, pater optime
> [divum,
> distrahis in casus? quo me parat alea fati
> perdere delicto? superi, quo crimine tantas
> promerui poenas?»

We last encountered the image of the dice in the speech of the mutilated prisoner Euctemon (6.244); and its appearance here recalls Darius' earlier musings concerning the fickleness of Fortuna. The complaint itself echoes that of Boethius in the *Consolation* regarding the punishments which afflict good men (4. pr. 5). In contrast to Curtius, who portrays Darius as unwilling to commit suicide (5.12.11), Walter has Darius attempt to kill himself after he convinces himself that his death soon is inevitable anyway (7.51-58). Foiled, he is bound and fettered. Curtius at this point makes a comment about Fortuna's devising mockeries for the king (5.12-20: nova ludibria subinde excogitante Fortuna). But Walter takes the opportunity to repeat his use of the dice as an image of Fortuna (7.74-79):

> proh quanta licentia fati,
> quam vaga, quae versat humanos alea casus!
> quem prius aurato curru videre sedentem
> et tremuere sui, iam non suus, ille suorum
> vincitur manibus et in arta sede locatur,
> captivumque trahit currus angustia regem.

Darius has been reduced to captivity among his own men by his defeat in war—elsewhere described as the dice game of Mars; hence his woes can be attributed to the unpredictable dice (quam vaga...alea). Alexander, of course, sees Fortuna at work here as always. When he learns what has been done to the king, he declares that Darius now has reached the «end of his Fortuna and his woes» (7.110: Fortunae finem metamque malorum).

Walter differs from Curtius also in details of his account of Darius' death. The king refuses to flee from the advancing Macedonian army even though his traitorous captors threaten him (7.185-194):

> ille venenosos monitus et dicta repellit,
> ultoresque deos testatur adesse, fidemque
> acris Alexandri lacrimis implorat obortis,
> seque negat scelerum comitari velle clientes.

> «nullus» ait «mortis metus aut violentia fati
> compellet Darium scelerum se iungere castris.
> non habet ulterius, quod nostris cladibus addat
> Fortunae gladius, mors, quam parricida minatur,
> antidotum moeroris erit mortisque venenum
> pro medicamentis curaque laboris habebo.»

Walter has invented the two references to poison (ille venenosos monitus et dicta repellit... mortisque venenum) and the phrase *Fortunae gladius*. The «sword of Fortuna» is an understandable image for a man who sees the influence of that divinity behind his defeats; but the «poison of death» is an odd phrase to utter just before one is stabbed. But this double mention of poison makes Darius' death foreshadow that of Alexander, who is to be killed by real poison. The connection between the deaths of the two rivals is strengthened in the following scene (expanded from Justin 11.15), in which Darius addresses his last words, through Polystratus, to Alexander. Darius says that the opportunity to relay a message to Alexander is the one consolation of his approaching death (7.255-259):

> Fortunae praesentis, ait, mortisque propinquae
> hoc unum Dario et solum solamen habetur,
> quod tecum mihi non opus est interprete lingua,
> quod loquor extremum discretis auribus, et quod
> non erit extremas incassum promere voces.

He praises Alexander, especially for his treatment of his wife and children, then asks that he punish Bessus, since Fortuna prevents Darius from doing so (7.278-286):

> his precor a iusto reddatur principe talis
> talio pro meritis, qualem parricida meretur,
> quamque repensurus, mihi si Fortuna triumphum
> concessisset eram: neque enim hoc discrimine solum
> alea versatur mea, sed communis eorum
> qui praesunt turbae et populi moderantur habenas.
> in me causa agitur. decernat pondere iusto
> Magnus, quae tantum maneat vindicta reatum,
> quae nova flagitii scelus expiet ultio tanti.

Fortuna has not granted victory to Darius. His dice are played (alea versatur mea); but this image occurs in a sentence which emphasizes that Darius' fate is linked to Alexander's (neque enim hoc discrimine solum...sed communis). While the substance of this message—the expression of gratitude, the request for vengeance—is taken from Justin, the references to Fortuna and the gambling image are again Walter's addition. Moreover, Walter links this speech, in which Darius ends with a prayer that the whole world be subject to Alexander (7.296: totus Alexandro famuletur subditus orbis), to that in which the High Priest of Jerusalem promises Alexander that same achievement (1.533: omnemque tibi pessumdabo terram). The language describing the sudden disappearance of the latter (1.535: superasque recessit in auras) is echoed in the departure of Darius' soul from his body (7.305: tenues evasit liber in auras).

Throughout the *Alexandreis,* Walter weaves together narrative and personal comment to create an epic operating on two levels. Before reporting Alexander's response to the words of Darius, Walter inserts a long apostrophe (7.305-347). He begins by attacking the same three vices about which Aristotle had warned the young Alexander—greed (7.310-311: funestus habendi / amor), lust (7.311: carnis amica libido) and drunkenness (7.313-314: obscoenus...venter / ...Bacchus). Then after several allusions to contemporary events Walter turns to the real subject of his outburst (7.332-337):

> sed quia labilium seducta cupidine rerum,
> dum sequitur profugi bona momentanea mundi,
> allicit illecebris animam caro, non sinit esse
> principii memorem, vel cuius imaginis instar
> facta sit aut quorsum resoluta carne reverti
> debeat: inde boni subit ignorantia veri.

In this passage Walter continues to refine the underlying theme of the epic. He is attacking the ignorance of the true good (boni...ignorantia veri) which results from the quest for the transitory pleasures of this world (labilium rerum...profugi bona momentanea mundi). The message of course is the same as that of the *Consolation,* and reaffirms the significance of the recurring allusions to that work. Nor does it seem unimportant that Walter has placed this clear statement of his intent at such a critical point in the narrative, with Alexander's great foe dead and «success» assured. We have here an example of the same technique which Walter employed in Book Five. At an apparent moment of triumph, he undercuts the quality of the victory. In Book Five, Walter points to Alexander's imminent decline from *virtus*; in Book Seven, he stresses the emptiness of the glory that Alexander holds to be the lone consolation of his mortality.

Alexander's speech concerning his dead foe is immediately preceded by the second of three instances in which Walter claims that his poetry will bring undying fame (7.344-347):

> te tamen, o Dari, si quae modo scribimus olim
> sunt habitura fidem, Pompeio Francia iuste
> laudibus aequabit: vivet cum vate superstes
> gloria defuncti nullum moritura per aevum.

The irony of this passage lies in part in the equation of Darius with Pompey; for Walter thus implies that Alexander is to be equated with Caesar; and, as I have said, the Caesar of the *Bellum Civile* is no *exemplar virtutis.* Moreover, there is in Walter's formula a measure of self-irony, since he has so skillfully employed reminiscences of the *Consolation* to belittle the transient glory that secular literature can bestow.

And yet glory, *vanitas* that it is, is the one consolation which Alexander finds when he ponders the death of Darius (7.354-361):

> ergo ubi purpureo lacrimam siccavit amictu,
> purgavitque genas: «miseris mortalibus,» inquit,
> «hoc solum relevamen inest, quod gloria mortem
> nescit, et occasum non sentit fama superstes.
> si vitae meritis respondet gloria famae,
> nulla tuos actus poterit delere vetustas,

> nec te posteritas, rex Persidis, inclite Dari,
> oblinet, aut veterum corrodet serra dierum.

The connection between Darius and Alexander continues. Alexander's opening words (miseris mortalibus...hoc solum relevamen inest) are the counterpart of those of Darius as reported by Polystratus (7.256: hoc unum Dario et solum solamen habetur). When Alexander ponders death, he is heartened only by thoughts of glory. In his view, glory does not die (gloria mortem / nescit), nor does fame perish (occasum non sentit fama).

The last major episode of Book Seven is the tale of the «returning home rumor» which Walter found in Curtius (6.2.15-3.18). In this instance he follows his model closely, since it already contains references to Fortuna and glory which are consistent with his development of those themes. Consider, for example, Curtius' version of Alexander's response to the news that his men are eager to break off the campaign (6.2.18):

> haud secus quam par erat territus, qui Indos atque ultima Orientis peragrare statuisset, praefectos copiarum in praetorium contrahit, obortisque lacrimis, ex medio gloriae spatio revocari se, victi magis quam victoris Fortunam in patriam relaturum, conquestus est; nec sibi ignaviam militum obstare, sed deum invidiam, qui fortissimis viris subitum patriae desiderium admovissent, paulo post in eandem cum maiore laude famaque redituris.

He complains that he is being thwarted at the mid-point of his glory (ex medio gloriae spatio) and will have to return bearing the Fortuna of one conquered rather than of a victor (victi magis quam victoris Fortunam in patriam relaturum). In the *Alexandreis* this complaint is given as follows (7.452-463):

> lacrimisque profusis
> limite de medio terrarum a civibus orbem

> auferri sibi conqueritur: virtutis in ipso
> limine Alexandro mundi totius apertum
> praecludi imperium: nihil in patriam nisi probra,
> Fortunam victi, se non victoris ad Argos
> esse relaturum: tantis obsistere coeptis
> invidiam superum, qui fortia pectora semper
> illiciunt patriaeque trahunt natalis amore:
> indecoresque viros sine nomine velle redire
> ad patrios ortus, indulto tempore magna
> laude reversuros.

Walter repeats the key statement concerning Fortuna almost verbatim (Fortunam victi, se non victoris ad Argos / esse relaturum). He keeps the reference to fame and adds the complaint that the soldiers are willing to return home *sine nomine*. Interestingly, Walter's version of «the mid-point of glory» is «the threshold of *virtus*» (virtutis in ipso / limine); but glory is the consequence of *virtus* attained. Similarly, though his version is much shorter, Walter retains the main thrust of Alexander's speech to the soldiers as given by Curtius (6.3. 1-18). However, where Curtius includes a reference to the insecurity of Alexander's conquests (6.3.5: si crederem satis certam esse possessionem terrarum), Walter adds a comment concerning chance (7.480-481: lubrica sors dederit: ergo si certa maneret / terrarum...). Walter likewise follows Curtius in having Alexander end with a successful appeal to the men's desire for glory (7.526-529). For them too it is a powerful force.

The narrative of Book Eight is dominated by two main episodes—the trial and execution of Philotas (8.75-334) and the conquest of the Scythians (8.358-513). The latter episode, as found in Curtius, fits the design of the *Alexandreis*; the former is adapted by Walter to meet his needs.

A hint of Walter's purpose with regard to the Philotas episode is manifest in the change which he makes in Alexander's speech revealing the existence of a plot against him. Curtius has Alexander begin thus (6.8.26):

> paene, inquit, milites, hominum scelere vobis ereptus sum; deum providentia et misericordia vivo.

Now the *Alexandreis* (8.98-99):

> paene, inquit, ademptus vobis, o cives, Fortunae munere vivo.

Earlier Walter had retained Curtius' reference to the «envy of the gods» (deum invidiam) when Alexander spoke (7.459) of the forces trying to stop him. Now Walter makes a change to reflect the continuing theme that Alexander sees Fortuna (Fortunae munere vivo) as a power constantly working on his behalf.

Fortuna figures prominently also in the *apologia* of Philotas. In Curtius' version he makes references to her at the beginning of his defense (6.10.2: inter optimam conscientiam et iniquissimam Fortunam destitutus) and near its conclusion (6.10.33):

> ego in ipso robore aetatis eripior, tibi carnifex spiritum adimet, quem, si Fortuna expectare voluisset, natura poscebat.

Walter retains the latter passage at the conclusion of his version (8.298-301):

> effeto sanguine patri
> spiritus eripitur, quem si Fortuna morari
> vel modicum sineret in obeso corpore, iure
> poscebat natura suo.

He increases the importance of the reference, however, by making these the last words uttered by Philotas before Alexander suddenly appears, and Philotas faints from fright. Likewise, Walter adds much more emphasis to Fortuna in the earlier portion of Philotas' *apologia*. Consider his opening statement (8.193-204):

> «insonti facile est» inquit «reperire
> verba: tenere modum misero non est leve, cives.

— 129 —

>   cumque sit in portu mens hinc mea, criminis expers
>   huius et in nullo sibi conscia, turbidus illinc
>   me tumido fluctu Fortunae verberet Auster,
>   inter utrumque situs, utriusque locatus in arto,
>   non video, qua lege quam parere vel huius
>   temporis articulo vel mundae a crimine menti.
>   forti Fortunae pereo, si pareo: mentem
>   non sinit insontem Fortuna potentior esse:
>   haec secura manet, in me parat illa securim:
>   hinc spes, inde metus: hinc salvus, naufragus illinc.

Philotas names Fortuna three times. The wind of Fortuna overwhelms him in the swelling wave (me tumido fluctu Fortunae verberet Auster). To obey Fortuna is to perish, for she does not allow him to have a guiltless mind. Indeed, Fortuna is preparing the ax against Philotas (in me parat illa securim). Moreover, all these references to Fortuna are bounded by images of shipwreck. Philotas begins by describing himself as caught in a swelling wave; and he concludes by saying that he is shipwrecked by Fortuna (naufragus illinc).

Walter himself leaves no doubt concerning the point of the episode. While describing the conspiracy which led to Philotas' downfall, he inserts an allusion to a twelfth-century scandal (8.168-171):

>   hoc habitu quondam Burchardum Flandria vidit,
>   solventem meritas occiso consule poenas,
>   quem rota poenalis tanto pro crimine torsit.

Rota poenalis is a marvelously ambiguous phrase. It can refer literally to the instrument of torture for the unfortunate Burchard; but it can also refer figuratively to the wheel of Fortuna. The latter notion is picked up in a second apostrophe with which Walter concludes this episode (8.323-334):

>   o quam difficili nisu sors provehit actus
>   lubrica mortales, et quos adscendere fecit
>   quam facile evertit! Magno Fortuna labore
>   fecerat excelsum media de gente Philotam:

> princeps militiae factus ductorque cohortis
> Parmenione satus, modico post tempore lapsus,
> scandere dum quaerit, fato damnatus et exsul
> obruitur saxis: certat simul omnis in unum
> volvere saxa manus, cuius manus ante movendi
> castra dabat signum. quam frivola gloria rerum,
> quam mundi fugitivus honor, quam nomen inane!
> praelatus, qui praeesse cupit, prodesse recusat.

Note the emphasis on Philotas' rise and fall (adscendere...lapsus...scandere dum quaerit); and consider as well Walter's renewed stress on the association between Fortuna (sors...lubrica...Fortuna) and the vanity of worldly fame (quam frivola gloria rerum...quam nomen inane!). The language of this attack on glory, interestingly enough, echoes the earlier statement by Alexander himself (2.484-486) in which he declares that he is satisfied with glory (mihi gloria sufficit) and loves fame (mihi nomen amo). Here, then, embodied in an episode ostensibly about someone else is another commentary on the emptiness of Alexander's goals.

Walter now turns briefly to Bessus, but again makes a significant change in Curtius' account. First, he jumps abruptly from the story of Bessus' death to the conquest of the Scythians, omitting the siege of Cyropolis. Seccond, he adds a moralizing tag to the report of the demise of Darius' killer (8.355-357):

> exitus hic Bessi: qui dum conscendere tentat
> labitur, imperium dum quaerit et imperat, in se
> regreditur, domini ponens insignia servus.

The language of this comment (conscendere...labitur...dum quaerit) reflects that of the apostrophe concerning Philotas (lapsus, scandere dum quaerit). This resemblance connects Bessus' fall, like that of Philotas, to the inexorable turning of the wheel of Fortuna. And this image serves as a fitting introduction to the long discourse by the Scythian ambassadors about Fortuna.

Walter's version of the visit of the Scythians to Alexander occupies the rest of Book Eight (8.358-513). Curtius' account of this event could hardly be more suitable to Walter's needs. The long speech by the envoy warning Alexander against invasion contains a striking portrait of Fortuna (7.8.24-25):

> proinde Fortunam tuam pressis manibus tene; lubrica est nec invita teneri potest. salubre consilium sequens quam praesens tempus ostendet melius. impone felicitati tuae frenos; facilius illam reges. nostri sine pedibus dicunt esse Fortunam, quae manus et pinnas tantum habet; cum manus porrigit, pinnas quoque comprehende.

Fortuna is slippery and cannot be held against her will. Without feet, she has only hands and wings—a difficult being indeed to grasp. Her image stands as a warning to put curbs on one's success. That Walter imitates this passage (8.448-459) and the whole speech is not surprising; but equally as revealing as his imitation are the alterations which Walter makes in order to blend this episode into the overall development of the Fortuna theme in the *Alexandreis*. For example, Curtius' brief mention of Alexander's ambition (7.8.13: sic quoque concupiscis quae non capis) becomes in the epic (8.377-379):

> vel si quanta cupis tantum tibi corporis esset,
> non tibi sufficeret capiendo maximus orbis,
> sed tua mundanas mensura excederet oras.

Were Alexander's body as great as his desires, the world itself would not be large enough to contain him. This description now both hints at the excessive ambition which will lead to Alexander's death and foreshadows the *sententia* about him at the end of the poem. Of interest too is an addition by Walter to the list of examples of «reversals» offered by the Scythian. Walter follows Curtius in noting that the lion becomes the food of birds, and rust consumes iron, but goes on to say (8.400-403):

> sub cardine Phoebi
> tam firmum nihil est, cui non metus esse ruinae
> possit ab invalido. quis non, dum navigat orbem,
> debeat occursum mortisque timere procellam?

Again the storm as an image of Fortuna: the man who sails the sea should fear the storm (dum navigat orbem, debeat... timere procellam). The man absorbed in the quest for glory and earthly success should expect reversals.

Of all Walter's changes in this episode, none is more important than those which he makes in the description of Fortuna (8.448-459):

> proinde manu pressa digitisque tenere recurvis
> Fortunam memor esto tuam, quae lubrica semper
> et levis est, numquamque potest invita teneri.
> consilium ergo salubre sequens quod temporis offert
> gratia praesentis, dum prospera luditur a te
> alea, dum celeris Fortunae munera nondum
> accusas, impone modum felicibus armis,
> ne rota forte tuos evertat versa labores.
> nostri Fortunam pedibus dixere carentem,
> pennatasque manus et habentem brachia pingunt,
> ergo manus si forte tibi porrexerit, alas
> corripe, ne rapidis, quando volet, avolet alis.

The beginning (8.448-450) and the end (8.454-459) of this passage are borrowed from Curtius; but the middle portion contains two striking innovations. The Scythian counsels moderation to Alexander «as long as he is playing a winning game» (dum prospera luditur a te / alea), and to beware lest «the wheel of Fortuna overturn his efforts» (ne rota forte tuos evertat versa labores). The reference to the wheel of Fortuna continues the series of allusions that begins with the Philotas episode. But note that Walter also inserts a reference to gambling. I have made mention previously of the importance of recurring allusions to the *alea Fortunae*. It appears in Aristotle's definition of *virtus*; it appears in a key passage linking the fates of Darius and Alexander; and it will appear again in the context of Alexander's view of life after death.

The focus of Book Nine, like that of Eight, is on two major episodes—Alexander's conquest of the Indian king Porus (1-325) and his own brush with death (326-580). In both episodes Walter has inserted elements which help to develop the theme of the inadequacy of Alexander's heroic outlook.

The key to the Porus episode is Walter's expansion of the dying king's message to Alexander. Curtius' version is rather spare (8.14.42-43):

> «quoniam» inquit «percontaris, respondebo ea libertate quam interrogando fecisti; neminem me fortiorem esse censebam. meas enim noveram vires, nondum expertus tuas; fortiorem esse te belli docuit eventus. sed ne sic quidem parum felix sum, secundus tibi.» rursus interrogatus quid ipse victorem statuere debere censeret: «quod hic» inquit «dies tibi suadet, quo expertus es quam caduca felicitas esset.»

Porus has learned that Alexander is stronger than he; when asked how he thought the victor ought to treat him, he replies «as the day advises on which he learned how perishable success is» (quam caduca felicitas esset). In the *Alexandreis*, Porus' speech is as follows (9.298-316):

> at Porus: «quia quaeris,» ait «respondeo tanta
> libertate tibi, quantam mihi, Magne, dedisti
> quaerendo prius, ante malum certaminis huius
> nemo erat in terris, quem posse resistere, quemve
> censerem mihi Marte parem vel mente, meamque
> vim noram et meritum, nondum tua fata tuasque
> expertus vires: sed quam me fortior esses
> eventus belli docuit: tibi vero secundus
> non minimum felix videor mihi. ne tamen isto
> attollas animum casu, quia viceris; ipse
> exemplum tibi sum: qui cum fortissimus essem
> fortius inveni. ne dixeris, esse beatum
> qui quo crescat habet, nisi quo decrescere possit

> non habeat. satius est non adscendere, quam post
> adscensum regredi; melius non crescere, quam post
> augmentum minui. gravius torquentur avari
> amissi memores, quam delectantur habendo.
> proinde tui cursus frenum moderare. caduca
> sunt bona Fortunae stabilisque ignara favoris.»

Walter's changes, as usual, are concerned with increasing the emphasis on Fortuna in the speech. Porus urges caution (ne tamen isto / attollas animum casu). Do not, he says, call a man blessed unless he is free of the danger of falling. Porus labels himself an *exemplum* for Alexander, because although strong, he found a stronger foe; and he warns that the gifts of Fortuna are fickle and «ignorant of steadfast favor» (stabilisque ignara favoris). As striking as the mention of Fortuna by Porus is the mingling of the imagery of the moon, through the notion of waxing and waning (crescat...decrescere...augmentum minui), with that of the wheel, through the notion of ascent and descent (adscendere...regredi), to emphasize her changeable nature. Moreover, the statement in which Porus declares himself an *exemplum* for Alexander foreshadows Walter's assertion at the end of the epic that Alexander is an *exemplum* for the reader (24). And we will see that, in Walter's telling of the story, the warning from Porus will prove accurate, even if there exists no mortal adversary who is *fortior Alexandro*.

Mentions of Fortuna serve as a transition from this episode to the next. Alexander marvels that the king's spirit has not been broken by the wheel of Fortuna (9.317-318: Fortunae turbine regem / infractum). But he is also elated because Fortuna has granted him so great a victory (9.329: prodiga tam celebrem dederat Fortuna triumphum), which seems to

---

(24) On the use of the word *exemplum* see J.-Th. Welter, *L'Exemplum dans la littérature religieuse du Môyen Age* (Paris and Toulouse, 1927); also useful is Goswin Frenken, *Die Exempla des Jacob von Vitry: ein Beitrag zur Geschichte der Erzählungsliteratur des Mittelalters* (Munich, 1914), pp. 5-18.

open the whole world to conquest. First the tribe of the Sudracae, who have barricaded themselves inside their city, must be overcome. The Greeks attack; and in the course of the battle Alexander alone scales the wall. He leaps inside and is seriously wounded by an arrow before the rest of the army breaches the wall and rescues him. The role of luck in this event had already been exploited by Curtius, who points out that Fortuna saved Alexander's life when he jumped into the midst of the enemy (9.5.3):

> sed forte ita libraverat corpus ut se pedibus exciperet; itaque stans init pugnam, et ne circumiri posset Fortuna providerat: vetusta arbor haud procul muro ramos multa fronde vestitos, velut de industria regem protegentes, obiecerat.

By landing on his feet Alexander is able to begin fighting at once; moreover, Fortuna had provided a tree close to the wall to prevent the king from being surrounded. Walter preserves most of this passage, changing it only to ascribe to Fortuna as well the fact that Alexander lands on his feet (9.374-382).

The victory won, Alexander is brought back to camp more dead than alive. Walter subtly weaves Fortuna into his account of the recovery of the king. The Greeks for the second time fear the death of their leader; however, the physician Critobulus cures him. To describe the feeling of relief which sweeps through the camp Walter uses an extended simile (9.493-500):

> qualis in Aegeo Borea bacchante profundo
> exoritur clamor, cum fracta puppe magister
> volvitur in medios everso vertice fluctus.
> fit fragor et similem timet unusquisque ruinam,
> seque omnes anima periisse fatentur in una:
> si tamen incolumem revocare tenacibus uncis
> et clavum reparare queant, sonat aura tumultu
> laetitiae, et primum vincunt nova gaudia luctum.

The distress of the soldiers has been like that suffered by sailors

when the helmsman has been swept overboard in a violent
storm. But if they are able to save him and pull him back on
the ship, then the air is filled with sounds of rejoicing, and
cheers replace laments. The image is both clever and ironic.
Alexander the helmsman is back to guide the ship. But the
army under him is still a ship at sea—that is, in the power of
Fortuna.

Walter also makes significant changes in two speeches
which occur in this episode. To Craterus' complaint about
Alexander's rashness Walter adds a suggestive reference to the
king's ambition (9.514-517):

>   «tua, regum maxime, virtus»
> inquit «et esuries mentis, cui maximus iste
> non satis est orbis, quem proponunt sibi finem?
> vel quem sunt habitura modum?»

Of interest here is the repetition of the themes of Alexander's
hunger for glory (esuries mentis) and the insufficiency of even
the whole world for his ambition (non satis est orbis). The
latter idea figures prominently in Alexander's reply to Craterus.
The greater part of this speech is taken from Curtius (9.6.
16-17); but as expected Walter gives greater emphasis to the
intertwined themes of glory and Fortuna (9.546-577):

>   «non minimum vobis obnoxius» inquit
> «aut ingratus ero, non solum quod scio nostram
> vos hodie, proceres, vestrae praeferre saluti,
> sed quod ab introitu regni vel origine belli
> erga me nullum pietatis opus vel amoris
> pignus omisistis. verum non est mihi prorsus
> mens ea quae vobis: neque enim desistere coeptis
> aut bellum finire volo, non me capit aetas,
> sed neque me spatio aetatis vel legibus huius
> metior, excedit aevi mea gloria metas:
> haec sola est, vestrum metiri qua volo regem.
> degeneres animi pectusque ignobili summum
> credunt esse bonum diuturna vivere vita.
> sed mundi rex unus ego, qui mille triumphos,

> non annos vitae numero, si munera recte
> computo Fortunae, vel si bene clara retractem
> gesta, diu vixi. Thracas Asiamque subegi;
> proximus est mundi mihi finis, et absque deorum
> ut loquar invidia, nimis est angustus et orbis,
> et terrae tractus domino non sufficit uni.
> quae tamen egressus postquam subiecero mundum,
> en alium vobis aperire sequentibus orbem
> iam mihi constitui, nihil insuperabile forti!
> Antipodum penetrare sinus aliamque videre
> Naturam accelero, mihi si tamen arma negatis,
> non possunt mihi deesse manus. ubicumque movebo,
> in theatro mundi totius me rear esse,
> ignotosque locos vulgusque ignobile bellis
> nobilitabo meis, et quas Natura removit
> gentibus occultas calcabitis hoc duce terras.
> his operam dare proposui, nec renuo claram,
> si Fortuna ferat, et in his exstinguere vitam.»

Walter takes almost verbatim from Curtius the language in which Alexander expresses his reliance on glory as the one measure of his success (mea gloria...haec sola est, vestrum metiri qua volo regem). Alexander argues that by this standard, and by the criterion of Fortuna's favors (si munera recte / computo Fortunae), he already has had a long life. But to Curtius' statement that Alexander wished to «open a new realm of Nature, a new world» (9.6.20: aliam Naturam, alium orbem aperire mihi statui), Walter adds the further ambition of reaching the realm of the Antipodes. Alexander's exclamation that nothing is impossible for the bold (nihil insuperabile forti!) is not in Curtius, and an allusion to it will occur in Book Ten. Also Walter's addition is the complaint of Alexander that the earth is too small for the conquest of it to satisfy him (nimis est angustus et orbis, / et terrae tractus domino non sufficit uni). The king thus confirms Craterus' suspicion. Finally, while Curtius' version ends with Alexander's injunction that Olympias be «consecrated to immortality» when she dies (9.6.26: mihi maximus laborum atque operum erit fructus, si Olympias mater immortalitati consecretur quandoque excesserit vita), Walter omits these words and instead focuses on the king's thoughts about his own death (his operam dare proposui... / et in his exstinguere vitam). As always, Alexander sees himself in the grip of Fortuna (si Fortuna ferat); but Book Ten will reveal a different power as the cause of his death.

Because Walter draws together in Book Ten the various elements which, when considered in relation to each other, provide the meaning that unifies the surface narrative, it will be useful now to examine the question of the structure of the *Alexandreis*. In brief, Walter has designed each of the succeeding books to build on the central themes which he establishes in Book One. In that book he presents the definition of the *virtus* to be pursued by Alexander, but also introduces the Boethian framework in which he will attack it as devoted to a false goal (glory) which places the hero under the control of Fortuna. In Book Two, Walter inserts the long speech by Fortuna which is modelled on her *apologia* in the *Consolation*; a second speech in that book, by Darius to his men, echoes Alexander's words to his army in Book One. Both generals speak paradoxically of their confidence of success despite their recognition of the inconstancy of the role of Fortuna in human affairs. The description of the shield of Darius, with which the book concludes, contains an important reference (2.533-534: proh gloria fallax / imperii) to the vanity of the prize which Alexander and Darius have both declared to be the goal of their lives. In Book Three, the contrasting situations of the two adversaries are used to explore the Boethian paradox that «Fortuna is more profitable when adverse.» The subject of Book Four is the battle of Arbela. In Book Four the major episode concerns Alexander's crisis of confidence, the resolution of that crisis by supernatural means, and Alexander's misinterpretation of the power which has helped him. In Book Five we see Alexander at the zenith of his success, but Walter threads into his account of the victory at Arbela ominous foreshadowings of the hero's fall and eventual death by poison.

While the first half of the *Alexandreis* ends with Alexander's triumphant entry into Babylon, the second half begins with a statement of regret by Walter that the king would be unable to withstand the *opulentia* of that city. Book Six contains the debate among the prisoners at Persepolis in which Walter has added greater emphasis to Curtius' comment regarding Fortuna as well as a strong personal statement, replete with allusions to the *Consolation*, on the fact that the Christian is aware that the power of Fortuna is illusory. The twin centerpieces of Book Seven are Darius' long soliloquy on Fortuna (in which Walter first uses the image of the dice to connect Darius and Alexander) and Walter's extended apostrophe concerning the ignorance of the true good which afflicts mankind. Finally, Books Eight and Nine both contain two major episodes which emphasize Fortuna: in Eight, the trial of Philotas and the embassy of the Scythians; in Nine, the death of Porus (who declares himself an *exemplum* for Alexander) and Alexander's near death. As I have shown, in all of these major episodes, when Walter inserts new material or alters his models, the result almost invariably is an increased emphasis concerning Fortuna—whether it is her role in human events as Alexander and the other characters interpret them or Walter's attack on the foolishness of that view. In sum, while the narrative focus may shift from Alexander to other characters, Fortuna herself constantly occupies center stage. The main characters of the *Alexandreis* all act on the belief that her operations are supreme. In this respect they differ little from the characters of the *Waltharius*. And like Gerald, Walter uses a skillful interweaving of narrative and sententious material to expose the falsity of that belief.

The subject of Book Ten is the death of Alexander. The key factors to consider in examining Walter's treatment are, first, the agents of his demise and their motives; second, Alexander's response to the fact that he is dying; and third, Walter's own commentary.

Alexander's death is initiated by Natura, who fears his considerable ambition. The importance of this innovation by Walter has been lost on previous critics of the *Alexandreis*. The mention of Natura is far more than a clumsy attempt, as

Cary labelled it, to follow the convention of including «divine machinery» in a Latin epic (25). To the contrary, the role of Natura in the death of Alexander is an allusion to Lucan's circumlocution, in his denunciation of the «mad son of Philip,» that only Natura could put an end to him (10.41-42):

> occurrit suprema dies, Naturaque solum
> hunc potuit finem vaesano ponere regi.

At this critical point in the narrative, then, Walter directs our attention to Lucan (26)—specifically to Lucan's attack on Alexander, a strange approach indeed in a work of panegyric!

To return to the story, Natura is upset by Alexander's own words (10.6-15):

> interea memcri recolens Natura dolore
> principis opprobrium mundo commune sibique,
> qui nimis angustum terrarum dixerat orbem,
> arcanasque sui partes aperire parabat
> gentibus armatis, subito turbata verendos
> canitie vultus, Hylen irata novumque
> intermittit opus, et quas formare figuras
> coeperat, et variis animas infundere membris
> turbida deseruit, velataque nubis amictu
> ad Styga tendit iter mundique arcana secundi.

With this development we see that Alexander's ambition (qui nimis angustum terrarum dixerat orbem) is to be the ultimate cause of his death because it will lead to the mobilizing of supernatural forces against him. Natura descends to the nether

---

(25) Cary, *op. cit.*, p. 183: «The conventions of the Latin epic and the author's personal inclinations lead to a misty mythology in the *Alexandreis*. Mars, Bellona, Victoria, Fortuna, Leviathon, Natura, and Proditio all appear in the text as personifications of various powers ... above all there is some single Power ... no Christian God ... it is some such impersonal power as stood behind Greek mythology.»

(26) Cary, *ibid.*, p. 192, suggests this allusion in a footnote but misses its significance.

world to enlist the help of Satan. Her argument that Alexander is their common enemy (10.28: nobis commune flagellum) has its basis in Alexander's own words. He had earlier threatened to storm the underworld to find Darius (5.252-255); and now Natura repeats to Satan Alexander's expressed desire to visit the land of the Antipodes (10.98-100):

> ni tibi caveris, istud
> non sinet intactum chaos, Antipodumque recessus
> alteriusque volet Naturae cernere solem.

She obviously infers that he intends also to attack the underworld (non sinet intactum chaos). She then appeals to Satan's reputation (10.101-104):

> ergo age, communem nobis ulciscere pestem.
> quae tua laus, coluber, vel quae tua gloria, primum
> eiecisse hominem, si tam venerabilis hortus
> cedat Alexandro? nec plura loquuta recessit.

What praise, what glory (quae tua laus...quae tua gloria) will Satan have gained from his victory over Adam if he loses to Alexander? The appeal to fame works. Satan's response is immediate and angry. He gathers together the denizens of Hell and addresses them (10.128-142):

> nam quis erit modus, o socii? quae meta flagelli
> huius? ait, quo cuncta tremunt, prolixior illi
> si mora pro libito frangendum indulserit orbem?
> ecce, sed id taceo, rupto parat obiice terrae
> Tartareum penetrare chaos, belloque subactis
> umbrarum dominis captivos ducere manes.
> est tamen in fatis, quod abominor, adfore tempus,
> quo novus in terris quadam partus novitate
> nescio quis nascetur homo, qui carceris huius
> ferrea subversis confringet claustra columnis,
> vasaque diripiens et fortia fortior arma,
> nostra triumphali populabitur atria ligno.

> proinde duces mortis nascenti occurrite morbo
> et regi Macetum: ne forte sit ille futurus
> Inferni domitor, leto praecludite vitam.

This speech, it should be noted, prompts Proditio, or Treason, to set in motion the poisoning of Alexander. In Satan's mind it is now definite: Alexander is planning to attack Hell, defeat him in war, and take prisoners! Indeed, he has heard disturbing prophecies of a man (nescio quis nascetur homo) who will overthrow the kingdom of Hell. Just in case Alexander is that individual, he must be killed. Satan is, of course, referring to the prophecy, well known to Walter's contemporary readers through the apocryphal Gospel of Nicodemus, of the Harrowing of Hell. But Christ, not Alexander, was the one ordained to wield the triumphant lance. How much skill at exegesis can we expect from Satan? Walter has made the death of his hero into something of a comedy of errors.

With the announcement by Treason that Alexander is to die when he drinks poisoned wine (10.148-149: dabitur liquor iste Falerno / mixtus Alexandro), Walter reintroduces the image of the king's «thirst» for glory. He then combines it with the themes of «sufficiency» and Fortuna to make explicit Alexander's inadequacy as an exemplar of *virtus*. Now Alexander is a wretch (10.171: miser), though his ignorance of the future (10.171: ignarus futuri) is nothing new; indeed, that ignorance was revealed most dramatically (5.241-243) just a few lines before he uttered the threat, which we now see to have been laden with irony, to follow Darius to the underworld if need be. The plans to conquer the rest of the world, Walter informs us, Alexander dared to conceive «in the citadel of his thirsting mind» (10.177: animi sitientis in arce); and this same image stands at the head of an apostrophe which Walter now addresses to Alexander (10.191-215):

> quo tendit tua, Magne, fames? quis finis habendi,
> quaerendi quis erit modus aut quae meta laborum?
> nil agis, o demens: licet omnia clauseris uno
> regna sub imperio, totumque subegeris orbem,

> semper egenus eris; animum nullius egentem
> non res efficiunt, sed sufficientia; quamvis
> sit modicum, si sufficiat, nullius egebis.
> o facilem falli, qui cum parat arma, paratur
> eius in interitum quod comprimat arma venenum.
> crescit avara sitis iuveni, sed potio tantam
> comprimet una sitim: nam proditor ille scelestis
> instructus monitis, ventis advectus iniquis,
> venerat Antipater Babylonem, ubi cum parricidis
> complicibusque suis facinus tractabat acerbum.
> quis furor, o superi? quid agis Fortuna? tuumne
> protectum toties perimi patieris alumnum?
> si fati mutare nequis decreta volentis,
> ut pereat Macedo, saltem secreta revela
> carnificum: potes auctores convertere leti
> et mortis mutare genus; converte venenum
> in gladium; satius et honestius occidet armis
> is qui plus deliquit in his. sed forsitan armis
> non potuere palam superi quem vincere dirum
> clam potuit virus. fuit ergo dignius illum
> occultum sentire nefas quam cedere ferro.

The first line, as I mentioned, picks up the food/drink image for Alexander's desire of glory (quo tendit tua, Magne, fames?). The phrase *finis habendi* implies that this desire is a kind of greed (cf. 7.310-311: habendi / ...amor). The *modus* and *meta* of the second line are echoes of the speech of Satan (10.128: nam quis erit modus...quae meta) which sealed Alexander's doom. The phrase *nil agis* is to be balanced by the use of *quid agis* to introduce Fortuna into the passage. The next five lines provide a clear statement of the meaning of the «sufficiency» theme which Walter has threaded throughout the *Alexandreis*. Possessions do not cause the mind to want nothing, but only sufficiency. In part this is a reiteration of the argument put forth by the Scythian envoy (8.425-431) that the greedy man always hungers after more. But the language of this passage, especially its joining of the notions of poverty (semper egenus eris) and sufficiency (non res efficiunt, sed sufficientia), establish the *Consolation* as its primary source (3. pr. 3):

> «qui vero eget aliquo, non est usquequaque sibi ipse sufficiens?» «minime» inquam. «tu itaque hanc insufficientiam plenus,» inquit, «opibus sustinebas?» «quidni?» inquam. «opes igitur nihilo indigentem sufficientemque sibi facere nequeunt et hoc erat quod promittere videbantur.»

Here we have a source of Walter's argument that however much he has a man who wants more is «in need» (*eget* in the *Consolation*; *semper egenus* in the *Alexandreis*) because he does not have enough (Boethius' *insufficientiam*; Walter's *sufficientia*). Nor does the resemblance between the passages end here, for Boethius continues (3. pr. 3):

> quis autem modus est quo pellatur divitiis indigentia? num enim divites esurire nequeunt? num sitire non possunt?... quare si opes nec submovere possunt indigentiam et ipsae suam faciunt, quid est quod eas sufficientiam praestare credatis?

Rich men too hunger and thirst; but their wealth cannot remove that want nor create sufficiency. Like Boethius, Walter links his discussion of sufficiency with a reference to thirst. But Alexander's is a figurative thirst (*avara sitis*) which the poisoned wine will quench (*potio tantam / comprimet una sitim*). I would note that the phrase preceding the mention of the *potio letalis* (*crescit avara sitis iuveni*) refers us back to the introduction of Alexander as a thirsting boy (1.30: *puer sitiens*), thus completing the ironic suggestion of the original phrase.

Quid agis Fortuna? Walter's complaint that Fortuna is unable or unwilling to change the instrument of Alexander's death serves as a transition to the next scene, in which Walter now completes the implied irony of another passage from the first half of the epic. That passage is the *laudatio* of Book

Five (5.491-520) which concludes with the suggestion that a contemporary king such as Alexander could effect the conversion of the entire world to Christianity. There Walter mentions first Carthage, then Spain, then «every people» (gens omnis). That list can now be recognized as a foreshadowing of the scene (expanded from Justin 12.12.1-3) in which Carthage, Spain, and at last every nation rush to submit to Alexander at Babylon (10.227...231...243-244: Carthaginis arces...Hispania...omnis in unum natio concurrit). But Walter immediately exclaims that Babylon was soon to prove fatal to Alexander (10.260: sibi fatales...proh pudor! arces); similarly the *laudatio* appears just after he has entered Babylon, the city which Walter points out was to prove the king's undoing (6.1-5). Thus in two related passages the poet undercuts the success of his hero at the moments when it appears greatest.

In Book Ten, as I said, Walter is drawing together the various thematic elements of his epic. Nowhere is his skill in this task more evident than in the simile which describes Alexander as he rushes to Babylon to receive the homage of those surrendering nations (10.249-259):

> Magnus ut accepit, quod confluxisset in unum
> ipsius opperiens adventum territus orbis,
> ardet adire locum mortis, remisque citata
> classe Semiramiam tendit festinus ad urbem.
> non aliter procul inspecto grege tigris equorum,
> cuius fulmineas urit sitis aspera fauces,
> excutitur stimulante fame, vivumque cruorem
> inmitis bibit et laceros incorporat artus.
> quam si forte sequens occulto tramite pungat
> cuspide venator, plangit fusoque per herbam
> inmoritur sitiens nec adhuc satiata cruore.

The *leunculus* is now a tiger, but still hungry and thirsty. But as Alexander is rushing to the city of his death (ardet adire locum mortis), so the tiger is killed by a hunter. This is the last of four extended similes likening Alexander to some kind of animal. Before examining this simile, I will first review the others. In Book Three, Alexander is compared as he hurries to meet Darius at Arbela to both a hunter and a hunting dog (3.454-459):

> nec mora, ne Dario regni penetrare liceret
> interiore sui, canis ut venaticus altis
> occultum silvis Actaeona nare sagaci
> vestigat, vel qui venator Gallicus aprum
> irato sequitur stringens venabula ferro,
> haud aliter Darium venatur.

In Book Two, Alexander in battle is like a raging wolf (2.398-407):

> sic ruit in praedam ieiuna fauce lycaon,
> cuius opem sicco mendicat ab ubere pendens
> vagitus prolis, tandemque impegit in agros
> caedis amica fames vacuis concepta sub antris.
> stat pecus attonitum, quod non fugere audet, et
> [ipsum
> si fugiat nemoris alios incurret hiatus.
> copula diripitur canibus, quos ore canoro
> et baculo et palmis irritat ab aggere pastor.
> haud aliter Macetum rex debacchatur in illam
> barbariem, quae nunc profugum pavitare ferebat.

The wolf pounces on the astonished flock (stat pecus attonitum) which is afraid to flee. The impact of this simile, I might add, is heightened by the fact that earlier in the same book (2.59-63) Walter compares the Persian army to a flock of sheep (2.59: balantes ad pascua veris iturae) whose shepherd is concerned—with reason!—lest a wolf diminish their number (2.62: ne minuat numerum lupus). The first simile, which I discussed at the beginning of this chapter, likens the young Alexander to a lion cub slaying deer in his mind.

Several observations emerge from a consideration of the four similes together. First, none of the images is unusual in the depiction of an epic hero; in fact, they reflect Walter's intention of creating a «classical» hero without Christian coloring. We can say that the similes point out how wrong Satan was in confusing Alexander with Christ. In animal terms, there is nothing of the lamb in Alexander. What the similes do establish is a link between the concept of animal violence and images of hunger and thirst. The first simile shows the lion cub licking his chops in vain (1.53: vacuum ferit improba lingua palatum); and we should keep in mind that this simile reinforces the picture of the young Alexander's thirst (1.30: arma puer sitiens) for military action. The second simile likewise emphasizes the hunger of a wild beast. The wolf is in fact a she-wolf, her children clinging to her dry dugs (sicco... ab ubere pendens). She is hungry-mouthed (ieiuna fauce) (27), and Walter notes that hunger is the companion of slaughter (caedis amica fames). It is interesting to observe, as we follow the progression of these images, that in Book Five Walter briefly compares Alexander in battle to a she-bear maddened by the loss of her cubs (5.184: advolat orbata catulis truculentior ursa). Also female is the tiger of the final simile. In this instance she is driven by both hunger (excutitur stimulante fame) and thirst (sitis aspera). Indeed, the last simile has something in common with each of the other three. Walter seems to have composed it as a summation of the animal imagery in his epic. The first simile pictures the lion cub spilling blood in his imagination (1.54: effunditque...cruorem), while the tigress drinks real blood (vivumque cruorem...inmitis bibit). She shares the hunger of the she-wolf in Book Two. The third simile introduces the hunter (venator...sequitur); and a hunter kills the tigress (sequens...venator). The death of the tigress is the element which separates the last simile from the others. The other animals, all images of Alexander in the midst of conquest, live. The tigress dies, for now Alexander is rushing toward his own doom. She dies still thirsty, not yet having drunk enough (sitiens nec adhuc satiata). In this too we will see that she is the image of the king.

---

(27) Cf. *Consolation* 4. pr. 3: «avaritia fervet alienarum opum violentus ereptor? lpi similem dixeris.»

Let us turn now to Alexander's own words and what they reveal of his attitude as he faces death. He delivers two major addresses in Book Ten, the first after he reenters Babylon (10.260-329), the second just before he dies (10.398-417). The two speeches are almost completely the work of Walter; taken together, they provide a striking portrayal of Alexander's outlook at the end of his life.

The first of the speeches contains an important passage which reaffirms Alexander's obsession with glory (10.314-319):

> eia, quaeramus alio sub sole iacentes
> Antipodum populos, ne gloria nostra relinquat
> vel virtus quid inexpertum quo crescere possit,
> vel quo perpetui mereatur carminis odas.
> me duce nulla meis tellus erit invia: vincit
> cuncta labor, nihil est investigabile forti.

This passage contains two echoes of the very words which have led to Alexander's death. He repeats his desire to search out the Antipodes and again utters his boast that nothing is beyond the reach of the bold man (nihil est investigabile forti). His impulse to action (ne gloria nostra relinquat...quo perpetui mereatur carminis odas) is still that reward which Aristotle had promised—fame. Alexander, to be sure, sees glory and *virtus* so closely linked that he hardly differentiates between them (gloria nostra...vel virtus).

As his previous words show Alexander still concerned with glory, the final speech shows that he is unable, even at the point of death, to turn his thoughts from the realm of Fortuna. With the exception of its first sentence, which is taken from Curtius (10.4.3), the entire address is Walter's invention (10.398-417):

> «quis, cum terris excessero,» dixit
> «talibus inveniet dignum? iam sufficit orbem
> terrarum rexisse mihi, satis axe sub isto
> prospera successit parentibus alea bellis.
> iam taedere potest membris mortalibus istam

> circumscribi animam, consumpsi tempus et aevum
> deditus humanis, satis in mortalibus haesi.
> hactenus haec: summum deinceps recturus Olym-
> [pum
> ad maiora vocor, et me vocat arduus aether,
> ut solium regni et sedem sortitus in astris
> cum Iove disponam rerum secreta brevesque
> eventus hominum, superumque negotia tractem.
> rursus in aethereas arces superumque cohortem
> forsitan Aetnaeos armat praesumptio fratres,
> duraque Typhoeo laxavit membra Pelorus.
> sub Iove decrepito superos et sidera credunt
> posse capi ex facili, rursusque lacessere tentant.
> sed quia Mars sine me belli discrimen abhorret,
> consilio Iovis et superum, licet ipse relucter,
> invitus trahor ad regnum.»

Alexander states that he is satisfied to have ruled the world, and has enjoyed enough success. Now his spirit is weary of being enclosed in a mortal frame, for he is called to greater things. He is to sit among the stars and with Jupiter dispose the secrets of the universe and manage the affairs of men and gods. Perhaps again the giants are contemplating an attack against Olympus. Because Mars does not want to face a decisive battle without Alexander, he is being called to help, even though he goes unwillingly.

Alexander's final hour is not tainted by false modesty. The ideas which he expresses are consistent with the values he has held throughout the epic. His opening expression of satisfaction (iam sufficit orbem / terrarum rexisse mihi) is the fourth such statement made by him. On reaching Asia, he had said that the conquest of that continent would suffice for him (1.440-441: mihi sufficit una / haec regio). Later, when exhorting his men, he declared that glory was enough (2.485: mihi gloria sufficit una). Later, however, the Scythian envoy asserts that Alexander will never be satisfied with his achievements (8.427: tibi pauper inopsque videris). Alexander's third statement then reveals how much his ambition has swelled since he first touched the shore of Asia. The hero who once would have found that one region sufficient now discovers that the earth itself is too small a domain (9.565: terrae tractus domino non sufficit uni). It is of course this excessive ambition, which Natura decides must be thwarted, that sets in motion the chain of events which make these Alexander's final words.

The gambling image which completes the expression of sufficiency in Book Ten (satis... / prospera successit parentibus alea bellis) has a two-fold significance. On the one hand, it harks back to the use of this image by Aristotle in his discourse on *virtus* (1.118: dum luditur alea Martis), and implies Alexander's belief that he has attained the pinnacle of achievement possible for a mortal hero. The same reference, on the other hand, has a second implication. For in the *Alexandreis,* as I have shown, Walter uses the dice as an image of Fortuna. Darius employs this image when he warns Alexander that he will come to a similar fate (7.280-284). The connection between dice, the wheel of Fortuna, and Alexander is stated with particular emphasis in the speech of the Scythian envoy (8.451-455):

> consilium ergo salubre sequens quod temporis offert
> gratia praesentis, dum prospera luditur a te
> alea, dum celeris Fortunae munera nondum
> accusas, impone modum felicibus armis,
> ne rota forte tuos evertat versa labores.

Alexander's words (prospera successit...alea) echo those of the Scythian (prospera luditur... / alea). By having Alexander use this image to describe his military conquests, Walter implies that his hero still sees his achievements as the result of the continuing favor of Fortuna.

Some parts of Alexander's speech may seem at first to reflect a changed attitude, even one of philosophic resignation (satis in mortalibus haesi); but here too the language invites a comparison between Alexander and Boethius, and that comparison belies our initial impression. Alexander is in fact not «satisfied.» He goes on to say that his death is not a departure from involvement in human concerns. To the contrary, he looks forward to helping Jupiter govern the *eventus hominum*. Compare this attitude with the argument of Philosophy in the *Consolation* (2. pr. 7):

> sin vero bene sibi mens conscia terreno carcere resoluta caelum libera petit, nonne omne terrenum negotium spernat quae se caelo fruens terrenis gaudet exemptam?

This is the passage which concludes the belittling attack on glory by Philosophy that I discussed earlier. She argues that the soul of the man who has reached understanding, when it is loosed from earthly imprisonment (terreno carcere resoluta), will rejoice in its freedom and shun any involvement in earthly traffic (omne terrenum negotium spernat). Not only does Alexander expect to continue his involvement in earthly traffic, but he also assumes that death will add a second level of involvement—with the affairs of the gods (eventus hominum superumque negotia tractem). Moreover, instead of rejoicing to leave this life, he goes unwillingly (invitus trahor ad regnum). Finally, in what specific *negotium* does Alexander expect to be most active? War. It would seem that he, like the tigress used to describe him, has not yet had his fill of blood. Through his use of the gaming image Alexander has reaffirmed the relationship of war and Fortuna; and that relationship now casts a special light on his concluding assertion that the gods undoubtedly need his military expertise (Mars sine me belli discrimen abhorret), the language of which evokes two other references to gaming—Aristotle's *alea Martis* and Darius' *neque enim hoc discrimine solum / alea versatur mea* (7.281-282). He is leaving life, not Fortuna behind.

What, then, can be said about Alexander's attitude? Certainly he has taken to heart Aristotle's exhortation to seek *virtus* in the attainment of glory through military achievement. But just as clearly he has been unable to transcend the limitations of Aristotle's teaching. He cannot envision even his after-life as anything but more of the same; and what remains the same is a preoccupation with transient goods under the sway of Fortuna. Alexander's words throughout the epic reveal little growth except in the magnitude of his ambition. Never satisfied, he seeks first Asia, then the world, which when conquered seems too small. Thwarted, he dies seeing death only as the entrance to another theater for playing the game of war.

Although Alexander's speeches in themselves provide a summation of the themes which have been developed throughout the *Alexandreis*, Walter nonetheless inserts one last apostrophe as though to insure that his message be understood (10.433-454):

> o felix mortale genus, si semper haberet
> aeternum prae mente bonum, finemque timeret,
> qui tam nobilibus media quam plebe creatis
> improvisus adest. animae discrimine magno
> dum quaerunter opes, dum fallax gloria rerum
> mortales oculos vanis circumvolat alis,
> dum petimus profugos qui nunc venduntur honores,
> verrimus aequoreos fluctus, vitamque perosi
> et caput et merces tumidis committimus undis.
> cumque per alpinas hiemes turbamque latronum
> Romuleas arces et avarae moenia Romae
> cernere solliciti, si cursu forte beato
> ad natale solum patriumque revertimur orbem,
> ecce repentinae modicaeque occasio febris
> dissolvit toto quacumque paravimus aevo.
> Magnus in exemplo est: cui non suffecerat orbis,
> sufficit exciso defossa marmore terra
> quinque pedum fabricata domus, qua nobile corpus
> exigua requievit humo, donec Ptolemaeus,
> cui legis Aegyptum in partem cessisse, verendi
> depositum fati toti venerabile mundo
> transtulit ad dictam de nomine principis urbem.

Walter begins by drawing a contrast between the true *aeternum bonum* and the transitory goods sought by mortals. In this context, he turns to glory, which for a second time (cf. 2.533) he calls *fallax*, thus echoing not only the words of the *Consolation* (3. pr. 6: gloria vero quam fallax saepe) but indeed the whole thrust of Boethius' contention that the desire for fame is *vanitas*. But that very desire and a commitment to the mutable world—that is, a commitment of himself to the power of Fortuna—are the two essential components of Alexander's heroic outlook. Walter now makes reference to Fortuna by means of an image which he has used before, that of mortals entrusting themselves to the sea (et caput et merces tumidis committimus undis). Then he draws everything together with a final mention of the theme of sufficiency (cui non suffecerat orbis). Now the earth, which contains Alexander's body, is no longer too small for him. In the midst of all this, Walter's reminder to us that Alexander is an *exemplum* hardly seems necessary. To be frank, I have long regarded it as heavy handed; and yet, given the number of readers whom the obvious meaning of the epic has eluded, perhaps it is excusable. The notion of Alexander as an *exemplum* draws us back, as did the reference to Natura at the beginning of Book Ten, to Lucan's denunciation of Alexander. It is Walter's last warning to the reader to look beneath the surface narrative, with its apparent praise of Alexander, and to perceive the real meaning of this ironic, Christian epic.

Like the *Waltharius,* the *Alexandreis* concludes on a joking note. Employing the topos of ending that «night is approaching» (10.455-456: mersurus lumina nocte / Phoebus), Walter adds the comment, perhaps inspired by the conclusion of Ovid's *Ars Amatoria* (3.809: lusus habet finem), that «I have played enough, now it is fitting to end the game» (10.457: iam satis est lusum, iam ludum incidere praestat). But has Walter finished playing? He continues with an odd circumlocution for «I am ready to turn to another composition» (10.458-460):

Pierides, alios deinceps modulamina vestra
alliciant animos: alium mihi postulo fontem,
qui semel exhaustus sitis est medicina secundae.

Walter has managed in this passage to attach to himself important elements of his criticism of Alexander. The gaming image (iam satis est lusum) calls to mind the *alea belli*. His claim to be satisfied is belied by his desire to begin anew, much as the dying Alexander looked forward to warring again. Walter even speaks of his poetic ambition as a thirst (sitis... secundae)! The last lines of the epic, addressed to Walter's patron, return to the theme with which the epic began—glory (10.466-469):

> nam licet indignum sit tanto praesule carmen,
> cum tamen exuerit mortales spiritus artus,
> vivemus pariter: vivet cum vate superstes
> gloria Guillermi nullum moritura per aevum.

This is the same formula, of course, which Walter uses to promise immmortal fame to Darius and Patron. In each instance the phrase calls to mind Lucan, the *Bellum Civile,* and the «glory» of Caesar. Moreover, the phrase *gloria Patronis* (6.510) is now revealed as a punning prelude to this claim of immortality for Walter's patron William. As I mentioned, the claim itself takes us back to the beginning of the epic, with its emphasis on the glory of Alexander. Between that opening and this conclusion, however, Walter has unleashed a clever and biting attack upon the desire for glory as vain and foolish. Should we not see, then, especially in the claim of personal glory (vivemus pariter) found in his last words proof that Walter, despite his assertion a few lines earlier, is not yet through with his game?

IRONY AND CHRISTIAN EPIC

Nor doth this grandeur and majestic show
Of luxury, though call'd magnificence,
More than of arms before, allure mine eye,
Much less my mind; though thou should'st add to tell
Thir sumptuous gluttonies, and gorgeous feasts
On *Citron* tables of *Atlantic* stone,
(For I have also heard, perhaps have read)
Their wines of *Setia, Cales,* and *Falerne,*
Chios and *Crete,* and how they quaff in Gold,
Crystal and Murrhine cups emboss'd with Gems
And studs of Pearl, to me should'st tell who thirst
And hunger still: then Embassies thou show'st
From Nations far and nigh; what honor that,
But tedious waste of time to sit and hear
So many hollow compliments and lies,
Outlandish flatteries? then proceed'st to talk
Of the Emperor, how easily subdu'd,
How gloriously; I shall, thou say'st, expel
A brutish monster; what if I withal
Expel a Devil who first made him such.
                    Paradise Regained 4.110-129

We have come full circle. Walter's comments concerning glory not only repeat the theme with which his own poem begins but also, by their emphasis upon the vanity of earthly fame, restate the argument used by Juvencus to justify the innovation of presenting Christian matter in epic form. The uneasiness which Juvencus felt about the compatibility of epic and Christian values was shared, I believe, by Gerald and Walter of Châtillon. The two poets lived centuries apart and wrote in very different circumstances; but it is difficult to imagine that either was «threatened» by the attractiveness of the *Aeneid, Bellum Civile,* or *Thebaid*—although perhaps Gerald would have shared to a greater extent Augustine's worry about weeping for the *errores* of Aeneas rather than for his own. Both men, as artists, sensed the inadequacy of the classical epic tradition for the expression of Christian values, and both demonstrate that inadequacy by ridiculing the notion of a Christian epic hero. The *Waltharius* and the *Alexandreis* are not attempts to resolve the problem which is exploited so effectively in Sedulius' *De Quodam Verbece.* Although Walter of Aquitaine and Alexander the Great are both superior men who are admirable in many respects, they are prevented from being worthy exemplars by flaws that are integral parts of the system of values by which their lives are governed. The poets seem interested not in offering balanced appraisals of «heroic» behavior, but rather in emphasizing those aspects most susceptible to Christian attack. Gerald directs his attack against avarice as the foundation of the Germanic heroic code. Walter is concerned more with the classical system of heroic values, and attacks the vanity of the search for worldly fame which it countenances.

Gerald regards glory and wealth as the twin motivators of the warriors in the heroic society which he is describing in the *Waltharius.* The goal of the heroic individual is to gain glory, that is, a reputation for excellence, through the performance of bold deeds. Material wealth is a symbol of the esteem which he has earned. The importance of these two factors can be seen in Gerald's comment that none of Attila's men dared to pursue the formidable Walter despite the desire to win through acts of valor long-lasting praise (411: virtute sua laudem captare perennem) and money-bags stuffed with treasure (412: gazam infarcire cruminis). Gerald paints glory as the greater of the two. Therefore, Walter fights to keep his treasure because he will suffer a diminution of his reputation should it be wrested from him. Moreover, acts of vengeance are required to keep one's reputation unsullied—or the reputation of one's lord, as is shown by Gunther's appeal to Hagen to enter the battle lest the Franks suffer an irreparable shame by losing to a single foe; and Hagen enters the fray with a declaration that he will do something memorable—that is, exact vengeance—or die.

Germanic heroic literature is filled with expressions of the sentiments which are held by the characters of the *Waltharius*. The two surviving fragments of the Old English poem *Waldere*, which was probably composed in the eighth century, contain the earliest written version of the legend which Gerald was retelling. There we find a similar statement that the warrior's duty is to distinguish himself by good [valiant] deeds (1.22-23: weortha thē selfne / gōdum daēdum). The notion that the warrior's two choices are death or glory is articulated with particular force in another passage from the *Waldere* (1.8-11):

> Now the day has come when thou shalt accomplish
> One of two: either lose thy life,
> Or win long fame, O Aelfhere's son,
> Among all mankind.

In like manner Beowulf argues that vengeance is a better response than mourning to the death of a friend, for by the former course of action the hero gains glory (*Boewulf* 1383-1389):

> Beowulf spoke, the son of Ecgtheow:
> «Sorrow not, brave one! Better for a man
> To avenge a friend than much to mourn.
> All men must die; let him who may
> Win glory ere death. That guerdon is best
> For a noble man when his name survives him.

The hero's duty is to avenge the death of a friend, as here;

or, as in the *Waltharius*, of a kinsman. Elsewhere in the *Beowulf* we can find expresion of the importance of treasure to the warrior as a material symbol of his excellence (cf. 2183-2196). But a passage of particular interest to the reader of the *Waltharius* occurs in the late tenth-century heroic poem *The Battle of Maldon* (55-61):

> Too shameful it seems
> That you with our tribute should take to your ships
> Unfought, when thus far you've invaded our land.
> You shall not so easily take our treasure,
> But sword-edge and spear-point first shall decide,
> The grim play of battle ere tribute is granted.

The essential point made here is that treasure given up without resistance brings little honor to the victor and shame to the defeated. The sentiment is similar to Walter's determination not to surrender to Gunther all the treasure which he has transported with such difficulty over such a great distance.

Gerald, then, is not misrepresenting the various elements of the heroic system of values. His innnovation is to subject them to criticism by suggesting that the desire for both treasure and glory is a kind of avarice. Gerald suppresses the importance of the theme of Hagen's conflicting loyalties, which presumably occupied a central position in the vernacular versions of the story, in order to emphasize the obvious greed of Walter and Gunther, and to accuse Hagen of it through the equation of avarice with the quest for fame. Gerald thus undercuts the heroic stature and pronouncements of his characters by exposing their values merely as manifestations of sinfulness.

To refashion the story of Alexander into a Christian *exemplum* it was necessary for Walter of Châtillon only to change the emphasis of two themes—glory and Fortuna—already prominent in the material which he inherited. Walter sees the pursuit of glory at the heart of the Greco-Roman concept of the heroic life. A name extended *per saecula* is the reward for excellence which Aristotle holds out to the young Alexander;

and the lack of fame after death is Alexander's one great fear. This desire for glory was a central theme in Curtius' account of Alexander's career, and Curtius emphasizes as well the role of Fortuna in his success. In addition, moralistic interpretations of Alexander's accomplishments—by both classical and Christian writers—had long derided his success as owed more to luck than *virtus*. Walter, however, uses the theme of Fortuna in a new way to expose the vanity of the search for worldly fame to which Alexander devotes his life. He is able to invest this old theme with new meaning by drawing on the attack in the *Consolation of Philosophy* upon Fortuna and those who submit themselves to her power. For Walter, Caesar's willing submission to Fortuna (*Bellum Civile* 1.226: te, Fortuna, sequor) seems to stand as a summation of an inadequate outlook on life. A Boethian framework ties together the otherwise episodic narrative, and is used by Walter to belittle the outmoded classical ideal of *virtus* and its goal of glory. Like Walter of Aquitaine, Alexander is guilty of a foolish absorption in temporal goods which blinds him to real values. And, as Boethius explains, those who set their hearts on a mutable rather than an immutable good have forsaken reason and have subjected themselves to Fortuna.

The influence of Boethius on Walter's thought can be seen not only in the *Alexandreis* but also in his shorter satiric poems. The seventh satire, for example, contains the following comment on the transitory nature of worldly goods (7a.6-7):

> omnis inest vanitas   mundi speciebus
> est Phebo mobilius   quidquid lustrat Phebus.
> alternantur singula   singulis diebus,
> ludit in humanis divina potentia rebus.
> mors inexorabilis   secum trahit optima,
> set nec parcit pessimis,   fert cum parvis maxima
> infimis sublimia,   summis equat infima,
> tendimus huc omnes, domus est hec ultima (1).

---

(1) Cf. the following stanzas from satires 4 and 13 for references to avarice and Fortuna. First 4.18:

This general statement on the flux of temporal affairs contains several images prominent in the *Alexandreis,* including the allusion to Fortuna's wheel suggested by the passage of time (alternantur singula) conjoined with the mingling of the highest with the lowest (infimis sublimia). Walter's use here of the gaming image (ludit in humanis...rebus) linked not to Fortuna by name but to the concept of a *divina potentia* is particularly arresting. The notion of death as the end of Fortuna's power is given as true for all; but we recall that Alexander's lust for glory blinded him even to this fact.

What is common to the attacks against the heroic tradition made in the *Waltharius* and the *Alexandreis* is a complaint that the «hero» is concerned with the wrong things. The glory for which Walter of Aquitaine and Alexander strive is exposed as a phantom, and their desire itself as a sinful greediness. Alexander knows no deity except Fortuna; and in battle Walter neglects the God he professes to worship in favor of Fortuna. War—or to use the descriptive Old English phrase *grimm gūthplega*—is, to be sure, the most fitting metaphor for their moral failure. It is a grim game (*Waltharius* 186: fraxinus et cornus ludum miscebat in unum) or even a dice game (*Alexandreis* I.118: dum luditur alea Martis). But as with all games of chance, the players are beholden to Lady Luck. So to Gerald and Walter the heroic warrior, whether his values are Germanic or Greco-Roman (and the two systems are in their essential nature indistinguishable), is immersed in a transitory world of gaming to the exclusion of the real world with its real life

---

quanto plura possidet, quanto plus ditescit,
tanto magis locuples sitit et ardescit;
nam sicut ydropicus, qui semper arescit,
crescit amor nummi, quantum ipsa pecunia crescit.

Then 13.14:

quid ergo Sciencie domum tibi struis
sapiens si pauper es, nec vales nec cluis;
set si ditat opibus te Fortuna suis,
diffusa est gratia in labiis tuis.

Note the appearance in 4.18 of the image of thirst (sitis et ardescit) applied to greed which Walter uses so effectively in the *Alexandreis.*

and death struggle for salvation. The two poets have adopted the conventions of epic narrative to attack the moral assumptions of that literary tradition.

Even though indications of the poets' ironic intent are readily available, both poems frequently have ben described as serious heroic narratives. In the first place, although an underlying Christian theme is not to be expected in every medieval narrative, we should be wary of discounting this possibility when the author is a monk or an accomplished satirist. With regard to Walter of Châtillon we can be even more confident, for (as I showed in the introductory chapter) his other poetry reveals a fondness and capacity for just the kind of sustained irony which he employs in the *Alexandreis*. When in the prologue to his epic Walter decries the tendency of people to condemn works capable of more than one meaning (prol. 12-13: et facilius sit ei ambigua depravare quam in partem interpretari meliorem), is he not giving a hint to the reader not to expect a simple tale?

What other arguments can be adduced from internal evidence? If the *Waltharius* and *Alexandreis* are not ironic but positive celebrations of heroic virtue, we must conclude that both poets have gone about their task ineptly. However, we know from his satires that Walter was capable of better, and Gerald takes pains to show that he is in control of his art. What are we then to make of the apparent inconsistencies within both epics? Let us take them as directives to thematic consistency at a deeper level. In the *Waltharius,* the apparent carelessness of the «catalogue of wounds» and the odd abruptness of the conclusion are in fact evocations of passages from the Bible and the *Psychomachia* which in turn unlock the meaning of the ironic sub-theme. Similar «carelessness» is observable in the *Alexandreis*. At the beginning of Book Six, Walter points to Alexander's fall from *virtus*. That fall is expressed in terms of his corruption by the luxury of Babylon, and makes specific reference to the vices against which Aristotle had warned: *luxuria,* drunkenness, and sexual attraction. Walter even anticipates this passage in Book Three when he laments the corrupting power of Fortuna on Alexander's inborn excellence. However, an examination of the remaining five books reveals no further treatment of this theme. Even Alexander's death, thought caused by poisoned wine, is not connected with an accusation of intemperance. Indeed, Walter's decision to pass over in silence the faults treated by Curtius has been used as part of the argument that he wished to make his portrait of Alexander wholly positive. But the question remains: Why does Walter mention these vices as the cause of Alexander's downfall if he is then going to ignore them? Even if corrupted to some degree at Babylon, Walter's Alexander does not fall from *virtus,* at least that defined by Aristotle at the beginning of the epic. Alexander's death can be traced to his insatiable desire for personal glory, an ambition which is given legitimacy, as it were, by the fact of its inclusion as the goal of a heroic life. I suggest that this apparent inconsistency in the *Alexandreis,* like that in the catalogue of wounds at the end of the *Waltharius,* is meant to give the reader two possibilities—a careless poet or a consistency at a second level of meaning.

Unfortunately, the predilection of many scholars to assume carelessness combined with their own carelessness in overlooking the subtle interplay of classical and Christian allusions in the two poems has made irony a feature of the critical reception of the *Waltharius* and *Alexandreis.* On the one hand, no Latin epic composed between the ninth and twelfth centuries, with the possible exception of the *Ruodlieb,* contains a successful portrait of the type of hero mocked by Gerald and Walter; indeed, that failure seems to reinforce the argument that the epic genre was ill suited to the portrayal of Christian virtue. On the other hand, the surface narratives of the two ironic epics have proven so attractive that Walter of Aquitaine and Alexander the Great are often cited as convincing examples of the very heroic type which they are intended to mock. In this respect, the reception of the *Waltharius* and *Alexandreis* is not wholly dissimilar to that of the *Consolation,* since Boethius' portrait of Fortuna proved to be far more beguiling a creation to later readers than his Lady Philosophy.

In the *Waltharius* and *Alexandreis*, then, we possess extraordinary examples of the use of irony sustained through an entire narrative; and a recognition of that irony is essential to our understanding of the subtle and complex artistry to be found in both poems. It is fair to say that Gerald and Walter are both playing a joke on their «heroes,» and that the fault is ours if we miss the point of the *ludus*. The *Waltharius* is, I think, the more effective work, perhaps in part because it is less difficult to maintain a mocking tone in a work of 1456 hexameters than in a work almost four times as long. I would not shrink from calling Gerald's poem a masterpiece of comic narrative. The surface tale is lively and engrossing; the sub-theme, hidden for a time but revealed in a way that allows the reader to congratulate himself for his own cleverness. The mocking tone which pervades the work keeps one constantly amused. But surely both poets deserve to be ranked among the best ironists of the medieval period. The examination of the *Alexandreis* lends support to the growing interest in the use of veiled criticism by twelfth and thirteenth-century writers of romance such as Chrétien, Gottfried von Strassburg and Hartman von Aue. In their detached and critical treatment of «love» and their use of irony to resolve the problem of the discrepancies between the conventions of the new romance genre and Christian *caritas* we can, I believe, see striking similarities with Walter's examination of «heroism.» Indeed, we should remember that the *Eneas* was composed at almost the same time as the *Alexandreis*. One genre which would produce the most memorable figures of late medieval narrative was being born while another, the classicizing epic, was being pronounced by one of its most skillful practitioners as a dead end for the depiction of exemplary behavior.

Yet I must emphasize, in concluding, that even in their mockery Gerald and Walter pay tribute to the vitality of the Latin epic tradition. No slavish imitators, they reshaped their models to new purposes; and in the course of exposing the inadequacy of the genre they produced two of the most successful and enduring adaptations of Latin epic. The *Waltharius* and *Alexandreis* are minor triumphs, to be sure; but it would tax the genius of Spenser and Milton to compose epics in which criticism of an outmoded *virtus* is subordinated to the larger purpose of forging the definition of a truly Christian heroism. Nonetheless, once understood, the use of irony by Gerald and Walter in their imaginative responses to the problem of the Christian hero is seen to be in the best tradition of creative transformation; and their achievement offers proof that some works of art can be taken seriously only with laughter.

LIST OF EDITIONS

Gerald: *Waltharius. Monumenta Germaniae Historica,* Poetae Latini Aevi Carolini, Volume 6, Part 1, ed. Karl Strecker (Weimar, 1951).
— Gerald's prologue: *Waltharius,* ed. K. Strecker (Berlin, 1947).
Walter of Châtillon. *M. Philippi Gualtheri Alexandreis,* ed. F. A. W. Mueldener (Leipzig, 1863).
— *Moralisch-satirische Gedichte Walters von Châtillon,* ed. K. Strecker (Heidelberg, 1929).
— *Die Lieder Walters von Châtillon in der Handschrift 351 von St. Omer,* ed. K. Strecker (Berlin, 1964 [1925]).
Vergil. *P. Vergili Maronis Opera,* ed. R. A. B. Mynors (Oxford, 1969).
Statius. *Statius* (2 Volumes), ed J. H. Mozley (Loeb Classical Library: London, 1961 [1928]).
Lucan. *Lucan: The Civil War,* ed J. D. Duff (Loeb Classical Library: London, 1969 [1928]).

CHAPTER ONE

Quintilian: *Institutio Oratoria* (Two Volumes), ed. M. Winterbottom Oxford, 1970).
Donatus: *Ars Grammatica,* in H. Keil, ed. *Grammatici Latini,* Volume 4 (Hildesheim, 1961).
Isidore of Seville: *Etymologiae* (Two Volumes), ed. W. M. Lindsay (Oxford, 1911).
Juvencus: *Evangeliorum Libri Quattuor,* ed. Johannes Huemer, Corpus Scriptorum Ecclesiasticorum Latinorum, Volume 4 (Vienna, 1891).
Sedulius Scottus: *De Quodam Verbece, MGH* PLAC, Volume 3, ed. Ludwig Traube (Berlin, 1896).

CHAPTER TWO

Prudentius: (Two Volumes, ed. H. J. Thomson (Loeb Classical Library: London, 1961).

CHAPTER THREE

Silius Italicus: *Punica* (Two Volumes), ed. J. D. Duff (Loeb Classical Library: London, 1927-1934).
Claudian: *Opera, MGH* Auctores Antiquissimi, ed. Th. Birt (Berlin, 1892).
Quintus Curtius: (Two Volumes), ed. John C. Rolfe (Loeb Classical Library: London, 1962).
Justin: *Epitoma Historiarum Philippicarum Pompei Trogi*, ed. Francis Ruehl (Leipzig, 1915).
Boethius, ed. H. F. Stewart and E. K. Rand (Loeb Classical Library: London, 1918; revised by S. J. Tester, 1973).
Geoffrey Chaucer: *Works*, ed. W. W. Skeat (Oxford, 1900).

CONCLUSION

Beowulf, transl. Charles W. Kennedy (New York, 1962 [1940]).
An Anthology of Old English Poetry [*Waldere, The Battle of Maldon*], transl. Charles W. Kennedy (New York, 1960).

Analytical Index

A

Achilles, 87, 89, 90, 109
Aeneas, 1-3, 9, 11, 12, 26, 28, 30, 31, 53, 55, 81, 92, 93, 158
Ahl, F., 77
Alan of Lille, 62, 63
Alexander the Great, 2, 12, 61-155 *passim*, 158, 160-164
allegoria, 2
Anderson, A. R., 80
Andersson, T., 16, 23, 32
annominatio, 66
Aristotle, 80-88, 92, 93, 117, 125, 133, 149, 151, 152, 160, 163, 164
Arnulf of Orleans, 4
Attila, 15, 21, 22, 26, 28-31, 33, 40, 41, 45, 47, 54-56, 158
Augustine, St., 18, 158

B

Battle of Maldon, 160
Benoît, 74
Benton, J., 3
Beowulf, 37, 159, 160
Bezzola, R. R., 63
Bible, 9, 11, 20, 31, 47, 48, 50, 58, 106, 163
Boethius, 18, 82-88, 90-95, 97, 101, 103, 104, 108, 111, 116, 120-123, 126, 139, 140, 145, 148, 151, 152, 154, 161, 164
Bolgar, R. R., 16, 63, 78
Boncompagno de Signa, 3
Brand, Jonsson, 63

Braun, W., 1
Brinkmann, H., 17

C

Caesar, Julius, 69, 73, 76, 77, 91-93, 126, 161
Carmen de Bello Saxonico, 1
Carmina Burana, 104
Cary, G., 63, 76-78, 141
Cesare, M. di, 64
Chaucer, 76, 84
Cherniss, M., 18
Chrétien de Troyes, 4, 5, 165
Christensen, H., 61, 63, 65, 74, 77, 78
Cicero, 3
Claudian, 70, 115
Corinthians II, 47
Courcelle, P., 84
Curtius, E. R., 36
Curtius, Quintus, 75, 90, 96, 98, 102, 104, 107, 109, 114, 117-123, 127-129, 131-134, 136-138, 140, 149, 161, 164

D

Darius, 65, 66, 74, 79, 94, 96-103, 105, 106, 109, 111, 113-115, 119-127, 131, 133, 139, 140, 142, 143, 147, 151, 155
Dido, 3, 26, 28, 30, 31, 54
Donatus, 3, 4
Dronke, P., 16, 30

E

Eberhard of Bethune, 62, 71
Ekkehard, I., 17, 23
ekphrasis, 65, 100, 105, 106, 109
Endt, I., 4
Eneas, 165
exemplum, 72, 73, 76, 78, 98, 100, 101, 114, 135, 140, 154, 160
Exodus, 50

F

Fortuna, 52, 72, 75-78, 83-85, 87, 89, 90, 92-106, 108-115, 118, 119, 122-125, 127-133, 135-140, 143-145, 149, 151-154, 160-162, 164
Friedman, J., 83
Friedrich, W.-H., 77

G

Gerald, 1, 2, 5, 8, 12, 13, 15-59 *passim*, 64-67, 69, 78, 86, 103, 104, 140, 154, 158-160, 162-166
Ghellinck, J. de, 63
Giordano, C., 63
Goswin, F., 135
Gottfried von Strassburg, 5, 165
Green, D. H., 4
Grimm, J., 16, 17
Gunther, 19, 20, 25, 26, 32-37, 39-45, 47-53, 57, 58, 159, 160

H

Hagen, 15, 19, 20, 25, 32-40, 42, 43, 45, 48-53, 55-58, 159, 160
Hagendahl, H., 2
Haidu, P., 5
Hartmann von Aue, 165
Haskins, C. H., 74
Henry of Ghent, 62
Henry of Settimello, 62
Hercules, 11, 80, 87
Hiltgunt, 26, 28, 34, 41-43, 45, 46
Homer, 6, 65, 89, 109
Huppé, B., 18

I

imitatio, 19, 63, 78

ironia, 2, 3, 4, 74, 117
Isaac, 11

J

Jakob von Maerlant, 62
Jerome, St., 10
Jesus Christ, 11, 19, 106, 116, 143
John of Salisbury, 61
Jones, G., 18, 31, 48
Joseph of Exeter, 62, 74
Josephus, 75, 90
Justin, 88, 122, 125, 146
Juvenal, 116

K

Karolus Magnus et Leo Papa, 1
Katscher, R., 16, 18, 32
Knapp, F., 63, 64, 71, 74, 75, 78
Krammer, H., 17
Kratz, D., 1, 8, 16, 74
Krause, W., 2
Kunzer, R., 5

L

Langosch, K., 16
Lewalski, B., 7
Libro de Alexandre, 61, 62, 63, 90
Ligurinus, 1
Livy, 75
Lucan, 4, 64, 65, 67-75, 77, 91-93, 115, 120, 126, 141, 154, 155, 158, 161
Luke, 10

M

Malkiel, M., 63, 90
Manitius, M., 61, 63
Mark, 50
Marrow, J., 10
Marti, B., 4
Matthew, 9, 51
Matthew of Vendôme, 62
Michael, I., 90
Milton, 7, 166
Miniconi, P.-J., 8, 23
Morford, M., 73
Morris, William, 78

N

Natura, 65, 72, 138, 140, 141, 142, 151, 154
Nibelungenlied, 15
Nicodemus, 143
Nigellus, Wireker, 62

O

Odysseus, 93
Ovid, 24
Owen, D. D. R., 4

P

Panzer, F., 23, 24
Patch, H., 77
Paul, St., 47
Pickering, F. P., 18, 77
Ploss, E. E., 16
Pompey, 68, 70, 126
Porus, 74, 134, 135, 140
Prudentius, 7, 11, 16, 18, 31, 33, 35, 36, 38, 40, 48, 51-56, 58, 163
Psalms, 9, 10

Q

Quintilian, 2

R

Raby, F. J. E., 63, 78, 80, 100
Reeh, R., 16, 17
Reinhold, M., 2
Robertson, D. W., Jr., 4
Ruodlieb, 1, 164

S

Schaller, D., 17
Schmeller, A., 16
Schumann, O., 16, 17, 18

Sedulius, Scottus, 7-13, 19, 47, 65, 158
Sheridan, J., 78
Silius, Italicus, 70
Smith, M., 7
Spenser, 166
Stackmann, K., 24
Statius, 16, 18-20, 23, 24, 64, 65, 68, 77, 158
Steinen, W. von den, 17, 18, 31, 32, 48
Strecker, K., 17, 62

T

Theodulf of Orleans, 7
Trogus Pompeius, 75
Turnus, 24-26, 53, 54

U

Ulrich von Eschenbach, 63

V

Valerius, Julius, 75
Venantius, Fortunatus, 30
Vergil, 1, 3, 4, 6, 7, 9, 12, 16, 19-31, 45, 47, 52-54, 64, 65, 74, 77, 91-93, 158
virtus, 2, 5, 36, 41, 81-83, 85-87, 90, 101, 102, 105, 111-113, 117, 126, 128, 133, 139, 140, 143, 149, 151, 152, 161, 163, 164, 166

W

Wagner, H., 23
Waldere, 159
Walter of Aquitaine, 2, 12, 15, 19, 20, 22-25, 57, 58, 158-162, 164
Walter of Châtillon, 2, 5, 8, 12, 61-155 *passim*, 158, 160-166
Welter, J., 135
William of Champagne, 62

SE TERMINÓ DE IMPRIMIR EN
LA CIUDAD DE MADRID EL DÍA
10 DE JUNIO DE 1980.

studia humanitatis

Louis Marcello La Favia, *Benvenuto Rambaldi da Imola: Dantista.* XII-188 pp. US $9.25.

John O'Connor, *Balzac's Soluble Fish.* XII-252 pp. US $14.25.

Carlos García, *La desordenada codicia*, edición crítica de Giulio Massano. XII-220 pp. US $11.50.

Everett W. Hesse, *Interpretando la Comedia.* XII-184 pp. US $10.00.

Nancy Dersofi, *Arcadia and the Stage: A Study of the Theater of Angelo Beolco* (called *Ruzante*). XII-180 pp. US $10.00.

Lewis Kamm, *The Object in Zola's* Rougon-Macquart. XII-160 pp. US $9.25.

Ann Bugliani, *Women and the Feminine Principle in the Works of Paul Claudel.* XII-144 pp. US $9.25.

Charlotte Frankel Gerrard, *Montherlant and Suicide.* XVI-72 pp. US $5.00.

The Two Hesperias. Literary Studies in Honor of Joseph G. Fucilla. Edited by Americo Bugliani. XX-372 pp. US $30.00.

Jean J. Smoot, *A Comparison of Plays by John M. Singe and Federico García Lorca: The Poets and Time.* XII-220 pp. US $13.00.

Laclos. Critical Approaches to Les Liaisons dangereuses. Ed. Lloyd R. Free. XII-300 pp. US $17.00.

Julia Conaway Bondanella, *Petrarch's Visions and their Renaissance Analogues.* XII-120 pp. US $7.00.

Vincenzo Tripodi, *Studi su Foscolo e Stern.* XII-216 pp. US $13.00.

Lope de Vega, *El Amor enamorado*, critical edition of John B. Wooldridge, Jr. XII-236 pp. US $13.00.

JOHN A. FREY, *The Aesthetics of the* ROUGON-MACQUART. XVI-356 pp. US $20.00.

CHESTER W. OBUCHOWSKI, *Mars on Trial: War as Seen by French Writers of the Twentieth Century.* XVI-320 pp. US $20.00.

MARIO ASTE, *La narrativa di Luigi Pirandello: Dalle novelle al romanzo «Uno, Nessuno e Centomila».* XVI-200 pp. US $11.00.

MECHTHILD CRANSTON, *Orion Resurgent: René Char, Poet of Presence.* XXIV-376 pp. US $22.50.

ANTONIO PLANELLS, *Cortázar: Metafísica y Erotismo.* XVI-220 pp. US $10.00.

MARY LEE BRETZ, *La evolución novelística de Pío Baroja.* VIII-476 pp. US $22.50.

Studies in Honor of Gerald E. Wade, edited by Sylvia Bowman, Bruno M. Damiani, Janet W. Díaz, E. Michael Gerli, Everett Hesse, John E. Keller, Luis Leal and Russell Sebold. XII-244 pp. US $20.00.

Cancionero del Bachiller Jhoan Lopez, Manuscrito 3168 de la Biblioteca Nacional de Madrid. Edición, estudio, bibliografía e índices por Rosalind J. Gabin. Tomo primero: LVI-368 pp. US $30.00.

DENNIS M. KRATZ, *Mocking Epic.* XVI-176 pp. $12.50.

EN PRENSA

Cancionero del Bachiller Jhoan Lopez, edición crítica de Rosalind J. Gabin. Tomo segundo.

HELMUT HATZFELD, *Essais sur la littérature flamboyante.*